A Texas Baptist Power Struggle

The Hayden Controversy

Joseph E. Early, Jr.

Foreword by John W. Storey

University of North Texas Press
Denton, Texas

Printed in the United States of America.

10 9 8 7 6 5 4 3 2 1

Permissions:
University of North Texas Press
P.O. Box 311336
Denton, TX 76203-1336

The paper used in this book meets the minimum requirements of the American National Standard for Permanence of Paper for Printed Library Materials, z39.48.1984. Binding materials have been chosen for durability.

Library of Congress Cataloging-in-Publication Data

Early, Joseph E. (Joseph Everett), 1970–
A Texas Baptist power struggle : the Hayden controversy / by Joseph E. Early, Jr. ; foreword by John W. Storey.
p. cm.
Includes bibliographical references (p.) and index.
ISBN-13: 978-1-57441-195-9 (cloth : alk. paper)
ISBN-10: 1-57441-195-0 (cloth : alk. paper)
1. Hayden, Samuel Augustus. 2. Baptist General Convention of Texas—History. 3. Baptists—Texas—History—19th century. 4. Texas—Church history. I. Title.
BX6248.T4E27 2005
286'.09764'09034—dc22

2005016502

For Dana

CONTENTS

Illustrations following page 96:

FOREWORD

Controversy seems almost second nature to Texas Baptists. When not waging war against external enemies from afar, they have often turned inward upon one another with unbecoming zest. At one point in the late nineteenth century rancor had produced five rival sate conventions, two hostile newspapers, and two competing universities. As Baptist historian J. M. Carroll observed, Texas Baptists had "created organizations within organizations—wheels within wheels—until one wheel could not turn without interfering with another."[1] So, in a sense, the Hayden controversy was just another Baptist slugfest, replete with strongwilled, uncompromising, and self-righteous personalities, charges and counter-charges, overblown rhetoric, and a pistol fight in the men's room of a moving passenger train.

This fine work by Professor Joe Early pulls together the diverse and complicated strands of the Hayden controversy and, significantly, treats the principal players as neither heroes nor villains. S. A. Hayden, certainly a contentious and divisive sort, emerges from these pages somewhat more favorably than usual, while B. H. Carroll, a giant among Texas Baptists, comes off as less than saintly, a man determined to have his way and prepared to behave in an unprincipled manner to get it. Basically, Early's study sheds light on a Texas Baptist power struggle involving ambitious men and a tug of war for denominational dominance between factions in Waco and Dallas. In retrospect, a rift between Hayden and B. H. Carroll appears unavoidable. Both men aspired to denominational leadership, both held strong views, and neither could succeed fully without in some way prevailing over the other.

If the Hayden controversy emanated from a clash of personalities, it quickly evolved into a bitter dispute over a fundamental issue of church policy. Specifically, what constitutes a Baptist convention? Hayden and his supporters believed the convention consisted of sovereign churches whose delegates could not be expelled from the annual gatherings. Carroll and his followers countered that the convention was composed of messengers selected by the churches, associations, and missionary societies, and that those messengers, when in session, constituted the convention, not the churches. Hayden's group lost this argument, and the upshot was the formation of yet another state convention, the Baptist Missionary Association. Giving his work a contemporary ring, Early draws an apt comparison between the Baptist Missionary Association and the recently organized Southern Baptists of Texas, a group forged in the heat of a current Texas Baptist battle.

Religious newspapers, which were then privately owned and reflected the opinions of their owners, figured prominently in the Hayden controversy. Through the columns of his Dallas-based paper, the *Texas Baptist and Herald*, Hayden verbally assaulted fellow Baptists with whom he disagreed. Located in Waco in 1892, the *Baptist Standard* afforded a voice to Baptists who took exception to Hayden. Early's investigation of this "newspaper war" has been exhaustive, and the result is the most balanced and fullest account to date of the Hayden controversy.

John W. Storey
Lamar University
Beaumont, Texas

PREFACE

Generally, Texas Baptists are known for two specific attributes. The first is evangelism. Wherever there are Texas Baptists one almost always finds a burning desire to lead the lost to Christ. The second attribute is not quite so noble. The Baptist denomination in Texas is also well known for its infighting. Whenever an enemy common to all Baptists cannot be found, the state's largest Protestant denomination inevitably turns upon itself.

As Texas Baptists enter the twenty-first century, they find themselves at odds with each other over doctrinal issues, the funding of their various institutions, and which group should speak for the entire denomination. Texas currently has two statewide organizations vying for denominational ascendency each with its own newspaper, its own leadership, and its own agenda. From Texarkana to El Paso and Gainesville to Brownsville, one would be hard pressed to find a Texas Baptist who has not chosen sides in this debate.

The most recent controversy erupted in 1998 while I was a student at Southwestern Baptist Theological Seminary in Forth Worth, Texas. An ultra-conservative group named the Southern Baptists of Texas (SBT) broke away from the Baptist General Convention of Texas (BGCT) and formed its own state convention. Though quite a bit smaller than the BGCT, the SBT has attracted most of the "mega-churches" in Texas. These very large congregations along with some 1300 other churches that joined them resulted in a reduction in the operating budget of the BGCT. Since its birth in 1998, the SBT budget has grown from $900,000 to more than $14,000,000 in 2003. This diversion of money resulted in several significant changes in the BGCT. While the budget of the BGCT for 2003 was in excess of $50,000,000 the organization still felt the monetary impact. The budgets for both 2001 and 2002 were under subscribed. Even though the BGCT enrolls more than 5,500 churches many of them are smaller and unable to increase their support significantly. Thus, the BGCT was forced to eliminate twenty full-time staff positions affecting several of the convention's services. The SBT, however, has too few churches and full-time workers to meet the outreach needs of its members. This lack of outreach is also complicated by the organizational structure of the mega-churches which are focused, for the most part, on meeting the needs of their very large congregations. Consequently, it appears that each faction as a result of the division will fall short of meeting the needs of all Texas Baptists. Since each group is incomplete without the other, this rivalry has the potential to weaken both organizations and eventually damage the Baptist witness in Texas.

While the formation of the SBT gained the attention of Baptists all over the United States, it deeply affected the students at Southwestern Seminary. Heated conversations and arguments ensued between students who found themselves at odds over the issues at hand. Despite these differences of opinion, everyone shared at least one common concern, "How is this going to affect Baptist life in Texas?"

Baptists across Texas knew this separation was about to occur. It was no secret. Since the 1994 firing of Russell Dilday as the president of Southwestern Seminary, denominational life in Texas had been strained. Even before the schism occurred, future leaders began to develop various arguments against the BGCT. In particular, this new group was opposed to the BGCT's position on certain ecclesiological issues, the dispersal of mission funds, the relationship to the Southern Baptist Convention (SBC), and the financial support of various denominational entities. Following the split, these issues, along with others, found their way into publication, the *Plumbline*, and the BGCT's newspaper, the *Baptist Standard*. From the inception of the split, these newspapers have been used by each group as a forum for debate and to attract additional members to their particular group and point of view.

Because of my love for Texas Baptists and concern over the future of the BGCT, I began to examine previous struggles in an attempt to determine how they ultimately affected the denomination. I examined several major denominational controversies that were centered in

Texas. I was then able to observe several historical trends, factors, and influences within these controversies that in one way or another shaped modern Texas Baptist life. Of all the denominational battles in Texas, one major nineteenth-century controversy appears to parallel many of the current issues. This affair was known as the Hayden Controversy. Since I found this episode so similar to current events, I undertook this work on the Hayden Controversy with the hope and prayer that my Baptist brethren across the state would realize the possible consequences of such activities.

Despite the severity of the current conflict, Baptist battles of the twentieth and twenty-first centuries are rather tame compared to the nineteenth-century Hayden conflict. Fraught with issues similar to those in our current conflict, Baptists of this bygone era battled with such ferocity that the denomination's very survival was sometimes in question. During this era rival Baptist groups fought each other for denominational ascendency on at least two separate but related occasions.

The initial conflict between rival Baptist bodies occurred in the earliest days of organized denominational life in post-Civil War Texas. The first group in this struggle was the older Baptist State Convention (BSC). Created in 1848, the BSC was centered in the south and Gulf Coast regions of Texas where Baptists found homes after traveling across the Gulf of Mexico from New Orleans to Galveston, Texas. Due to hostile native raids, it was not safe to travel overland through Oklahoma and Arkansas to Texas. Thus, the Baptist population in Texas, as well as the general population, was strongest in these regions. The BSC's capital was Independence in Washington County, Baylor University at Independence was its primary educational institution, and initially the *Texas Baptist* was its periodical. As loyaties shifted throughout the last quarter of the nineteenth century, the *Texas Baptist* was realigned with the Baptist General Association (BGA) in 1875. The BSC claimed several prominent Baptist leaders, including R. E. B. Baylor, William Tryon, James Huckins, and Z. N. Morrell.

The second group was the Baptist General Association (BGA). Born in 1868 out of the belief that the BSC leadership was ignoring many of its more distant members, the BGA was strongest in central and northeast Texas. Following the Civil War it became much safer to travel overland, and the population of these regions boomed. The BGA's capital was Waco in McLennan County, Waco University became its primary educational institution, and initially the *Texas Baptist Herald* was its primary newspaper. In a manner similar to the *Texas Baptist,* ever-changing loyalties led to the realignment of the *Baptist Herald* with the BSC in 1881. After the *Texas Baptist* and and the *Baptist Herald* were consolidated in 1886, the new periodical was named the *Texas Baptist and Herald.*

Though the BSC and the BGA were the largest and most developed Baptist associations in Texas, three other associations joined them on the mission field. Created out of the belief that neither of these bodies was ministering to their congregants, the East Texas Baptist Convention (1877–1884), the North Texas Missionary Baptist Convention (1879–1883), and the Central Texas Baptist Convention (1880–1884) emerged to fill this void. But these three bodies struggled financially and numerically and finally joined the BSC.

Though these five associations claimed distinct regions of Texas as their territories, their unofficial boundaries went largely ignored. The efforts of ministers, missionaries, and fundraisers frequently overlapped as they competed against one another for denominational leadership. This constant rubbing against each other led to problems. Some members of a church might be loyal to one convention, while other members aligned themselves with one of the others. The same problem occurred within the associations. By and large, the associations aligned themselves with one of the larger conventions. If a church did not want to support the convention its association had selected, it would either be ostracized or forced out of the association. Fragmentation and rivalry ruled the day. Following years of conflict, this painful ordeal appeared to come to an end in 1886 with the consolidation of these bodies into the Baptist General Convention of Texas. Hard feelings remained, however, and it took little provocation for them to once again rise to the surface.

Following the union of these former rivals, the BGCT built its power base in Waco, the *Baptist Standard* became its preferred periodical, and Baylor University at Waco was its pride and joy. Shortly after the birth of the BGCT, however, a new Baptist confrontation unfolded. The BGCT found itself at odds with a splinter group led by *Texas Baptist Herald* editor, Samuel Augustus Hayden. Disagreeing with the BGCT on doctrinal, regional, and personal matters, Hayden's constituency was almost exclusively located in east Texas. This faction's greatest strength and source of support were derived from Hayden's powerful newspaper, which was renamed the *Texas Baptist and Herald* in 1886. During the final decade of the nineteenth century virtually every leader within the denomination chose sides and fought with newspapers, in courtrooms, and at times with guns. Eventually those who supported Hayden left the BGCT and formed the Baptist Missionary Association (BMA) in 1901.

Since the Hayden Controversy led to open hostility and eventual schism, it is surprising that so little attention has been devoted to this event. Historians have written on specific aspects of the Hayden Controversy, but no one has dealt comprehensively with the topic in one work. Primary sources are available in the various Baptist newspapers, early Texas Baptist histories, and the memoirs of participants, but for one reason or another they have gone largely unexamined until now. With a new, but similar episode taking place in Texas, the Hayden Controversy deserves a fresh examination. At this point the words of philosopher George Santayana seem appropriate: "Those who do not learn from history are doomed to repeat it."

CHAPTER 1

PROBLEMS ON THE HORIZON

THE NINETEENTH CENTURY WAS a time of religious foment in the United States. The disestablishment that had accompanied the American Revolution meant that previously unfavorable religious bodies such as Baptists and Methodists were now free to compete with one and all for converts. As a result of this freedom, Baptists, Methodists, and, later, Cumberland Presbyterians, the various Christian churches, and Roman Catholics grew by leaps and bounds. One reason in particular for the growth of Baptists was the concept of congregational polity. Baptists believe that no organization supersedes the local church, and thus the membership of each local church chooses its own leaders and makes its own decisions. All affiliation with other Baptist churches from the national to the local level is on a voluntary basis. The Southern Baptist Convention, therefore, is composed of Baptist churches that have decided to freely associate with one another in order to pool their resources to promote various endeavors. However, with no hierarchy in place, the Baptist denomination has often found it difficult to discipline fellow churches that choose to associate, but are also divisive and whose actions are detrimental to the entire Convention. At the state level, nowhere has this problem been more prominent than in the Baptist General Convention of Texas, a body that has known bitter controversy.

Baptist Rivalries

During the early 1820s the first known Baptists arrived in a region of northern Mexico known as Texas. Due to the great danger of hostile Native American attacks on groups traveling overland, the most popular route to this new land was by way of the Gulf of Mexico. These earliest Baptists frequently traveled by ship from New Orleans to the deep seaport of Galveston. For this reason, the strongest presence of Baptists in Texas was originally in the south. Within a decade of their settlement in these regions, cities such as Independence, Washington-on-the-Brazos, Houston, and Galveston became hubs of the Baptist denomination. By the close of the 1830s, thousands of Baptists had migrated to these cities and surrounding areas.

Known for a desire to work together in missionary endeavors and to promote education for the clergy, these first Baptists formed the Union Association in 1840 and Baylor University at Independence in 1845. With their numbers growing rapidly, Baptists organized the Baptist State Convention (BSC) in 1848. Through these three organizations Baptists were able to gain an early denominational foothold on the southern regions of the state. Though little attention was paid to the sparsely populated northern and eastern sections, this organization was the first statewide Baptist convention in Texas.

By the 1850s the land route through Arkansas became safer, and Baptists began to migrate into the northeastern regions of the Lone Star State. By the end of the decade the old passage from New Orleans to Galveston had given way to the less expensive but more time-consuming wagon trails that led from Arkansas and the Oklahoma Territory to northeast Texas. This change not only increased tremendously the Baptists of north and central Texas, but also set the stage for denominational bickering. Although more Baptists now resided in the northern and central sections of Texas, leadership, funds, education, and missionary activity remained centered in south Texas. This caused the Baptists of north and east Texas to feel ignored, thus prompting them to create their own convention, one more attentive to their geographical area. The upshot was the East Baptist Convention, formed in 1855. This organization was renamed the Baptist General Association (BGA) in 1868. These disgruntled Baptists also created Waco University in 1858. And with these developments a new group of Baptist leaders began to move to the forefront in Texas.

It was not long before the two Baptist conventions and their leaders, having no common foe or threat to unite them and hold them together, found themselves at odds. Arguments over which group held dominion over certain regions soon began to dominate the various Baptist newspapers. Furthermore, a strong rivalry between Baylor University at Independence and Waco University began to develop. In an attempt to raise funds for their respective schools, supporters of the two fledgling universities promoted the merit of their own institution and berated the value of the other. Therefore, within a mere forty years of the arrival of their first numbers, Baptists in Texas found themselves plagued by infighting, a lack of cooperation, and confusion.

The final decades of the nineteenth century were both an exciting and problematic time for Texas Baptists. There was a change in leadership as death claimed the pathfinders of the Baptist State Convention (BSC), Zacharias M. Morrell (1803–1883), Robert Emmett Bledsoe Baylor (1793–1873), and William Tryon (1809–1847). This made way for a new group of gifted ministers with a great vision, men such as Benajah H. Carroll (1843–1914), James Milton Carroll (1852–1931), Robert Cooke Buckner (1833–1919), James Britton Cranfill (1858–1942), and James Bruton Gambrell (1841–1921). The foremost leader of this group would prove to be B. H. Carroll. Building upon the foundation left to them by their predecessors, this second generation of Baptist leaders sought to forge a unified denomination in a manner they believed to be the most prudent to the statewide Baptist effort. The most significant realization of their dreams occurred in 1886 with the creation of the Baptist General Convention of Texas.

Despite the optimism and unparalleled accomplishments of this period, 1886 to 1900 were years marked by personal squabbles between these men and those who felt slighted and dominated by their overwhelming presence. At times these fights were so severe that they threatened to destroy the very foundation of the BGCT before it could take a firm root. Because of the controversy in Texas, Baptists in the Lone Star State became somewhat insulated from Baptist affairs at the national level. With the possible exception of the Whitsitt Controversy, taking care of matters at home took precedence. During this era Samuel Augustus Hayden stood at the center of many of these Texas imbroglios, and his antics demanded the complete attention of the fledgling Baptist General Convention of Texas' leadership.

Struggles in the Methodist Church and Christian Church

The Baptists were not the only denomination in Texas to face debilitating internecine struggles. Following the years of Reconstruction, Texas branches of the Methodist church and Christian churches were also struggling to define themselves and their faith. Unlike the conflict in the BGCT, which was confined to Texas, the struggles of these other Protestant denominations were also fought at the national level.

The Methodist Church was struggling over the Wesleyan concept of Christian perfection and its offspring, the so-called Holiness Movement. John Wesley, the founder of Methodism, taught that after justification one had just begun the process of salvation. A person should strive for perfection by living a godly life. The process was a joint effort between the individual and God who granted perfection. In order to help a person toward perfection, God often granted the person more grace in the gift of the "second blessing." The fruits of the second blessing often manifested themselves in faith healings, communal living, and *glossolalai* (speaking in tongues). Those who initiated these beliefs became the core of what became known as the Holiness Movement. [1]

Methodist churches all over the United States were in dissension over how sanctification should be taught, promoted, or even if it should be avoided altogether. The primary problem could be found in the grandiose assertions of perfection and the self-perceived godliness of those who claimed to have received the second blessing. Those who had not received it, or rejected the concept of perfection, found its adherents arrogant and full of spiritual pride.

The Holiness Movement first appeared in Texas at Corsicana in the mid-1870s. At Corsicana, Reverend William Brush held a camp meeting in which faith healings and glossolalia were present. At Belton, Mrs. Martha McWhirter organized a commune in 1879 where women separated themselves from other non-sanctificationist Methodists so as to better seek perfection. The movement had gained such a strong following that the Northwest Texas Holiness Association was formed in 1883.

The outbreak of perfectionism in their conferences concerned the more conservative Texas Methodists. The movement was belittled by its detractors and especially the editors of the Texas-based *Christian Advocate.* The Northwest Conference then informed its ministers that they were to report any of their congregants who espoused Holiness teachings and inclinations. In 1897 the Northwest Conference petitioned the national General Conference to issue a dictum forbidding traveling preachers to hold Holiness meetings within its bounds. The North Texas Conference had passed a similar resolution in 1895 that denounced the movement and told conference pastors to discourage it by any means possible.[2] The threat, however, began to dissipate before official action at the national level became necessary.

With the conclusion of the nineteenth century, the arguments over the Holiness Movement within Methodist churches began to settle down all over the nation. Tiring of conference belittlement and confrontation, the majority of Holiness churches in Texas left the denomination and became independent Methodist churches. Others joined the more open Methodist Episcopal Church. In 1900 still another group consisting of twenty churches in the region of Van Alstyne, Texas, became members of a non-binding association called the Independent Holiness Church.[3] The Methodist Church in Texas never completely recovered from the desertion of so many of its churches.

The Christian Church, or as they are more widely known, the Disciples of Christ, were also going through a debilitating split on a national level in the 1880s. Founded by Barton Stone and Alexander Campbell in 1832, the doctrine of the Christian Church sought to return to the Christianity of the New Testament period. For this reason, members did not allow for the implementation of any element into their worship services that was not strictly ordained by the Bible. Their famous motto was "Where the Bible speaks, we speak. Where the Bible is silent, we are silent."

On a national level, Christian Church congregations began to split in 1862 over the implementation of missionary organizations, musical instruments in worship, and the move away from a literal interpretation of the Bible. A denominational schism over these issues occurred in 1906. The conservative churches took the title Churches of Christ, and the more progressive churches retained the name Christian Church.

Within ten years of the close of the Civil War such differences of opinion on doctrine appeared in Texas. Problems, however, progressed more quickly in Texas than they had on the national level. By 1872 arguments between the more conservative and progressive Christian Churches in Texas had led to congregational splits in Waco, Dallas, and Waxahachie. Preceding the national split by twenty years, a formal statewide division of the Christian Church took place at Austin in 1886. The final break occurred because the progressives wanted to create the Texas Christian Missionary Society to help facilitate evangelism in Texas and introduce musical instruments into worship. The conservative delegates opposed the Society because of their belief that no organization should supercede the local church and that the use of musical instruments in worship was unbiblical. As would later be echoed on the national level, those who maintained a strict interpretation of the Bible became known as the Churches of Christ. Those congregations that maintained a progressive theology retained the title Christian Church.[4] This schism damaged the growth and viability of both denominations in the final decade of the nineteenth century.

Thus, during this period in Texas, the Methodists, the various branches of the Churches of Christ, and the Baptists struggled in their efforts to redefine themselves to meet the needs of a modern society and away from those of a raw and untamed frontier. Old habits died hard and those related to religious life in Texas were no exception. These changes were bound to face resistance, in particular given the interests of many to define new seats of power and to follow denominational leaders.

Hayden and the Baptist Situation

Among Texas Baptists, the man at the center of the storm was Samuel Augustus Hayden (1839-1918). He was born in Washington Parish, Louisiana, on April 7, 1839. The son of a school teacher and planter, Hayden lived on the family's farm in Washington, Louisiana, until the age of fourteen. He then attended the Floridian Male Academy in Greensburg, Louisiana. After high school Hayden attended Georgetown College, Kentucky, in 1857. He then pursued a ministerial degree at Southwestern Theological Seminary, the ministerial wing of Georgetown College.[5]

Before he completed his degree, the Civil War began and Hayden joined the Confederate army's Sixteenth Louisiana Infantry, which belonged to the Army of Tennessee.[6] Serving as a captain, he participated in several important battles, including Shiloh and Chickamauga. In 1864 Hayden was captured as a spy after the Battle of Nashville and spent the remainder of the war as a prisoner. While a prisoner, Hayden made clear that as long as there was an organized military resistance to the North, he would continue to fight. Because of such defiance, he was among the last prisoners to be freed. He was finally released in July 1865.[7] When asked about Hayden's military service, General Randall Lee Gibson, his commander, stated: "I never had the honor to command a braver or more skillful soldier. There was no officer of his rank in the Army of Tennessee more conspicuous for daring, skill, modesty, and Christian virtues than Captain Hayden."[8]

Following the war Hayden briefly served as an editor in New York before returning in the fall of 1866 to Louisiana, where he was ordained to the gospel ministry. For the next two years he taught Latin, Greek, and advanced mathematics at the Floridian Classical Academy while concurrently editing the local newspaper, *The Star and Journal,* in Greensburg, Louisiana. Hayden's ministerial career began in 1868, when he became the pastor of the First Baptist Church of Clinton, Louisiana. A five-year stay here was followed by a call as pastor of the First Baptist Church of New Orleans. In 1875 Hayden moved to Texas, where he became the pastor of the First Baptist Church of Paris. After a year in Paris he accepted a call to pastor the Broadway Baptist Church in Galveston, Texas.[9] During these tenures Hayden claimed to have healed ruptures within his respective congregations.[10] While in Paris and Galveston, Hayden served as the vice president of the Baptist General Association in both 1877 and 1878 and delivered the associational sermon in 1879. In 1881 he was awarded an honorary doctor of divinity degree by Waco University. Hence, as of 1881, Hayden appeared to be a well educated and deeply respected Texas Baptist minister. As of yet there were no marks on his ministerial character.

Hayden was called to pastor the Live Oak Baptist Church of Dallas in 1883.[11] Upon his arrival he found the congregation embittered and in disarray. The majority of the congregation was composed of former discontented members from the First Baptist Church who had either withdrawn or been expelled from the membership. There can be little doubt that the rupture that had taken place within the First Baptist Church had left hard feelings between the estranged congregations. The state of affairs was volatile at best. Hayden, therefore, did not create the situation that awaited him. Yet, since the First Baptist Church of Dallas was closely aligned with the Baptist General Association, Hayden, as an executive in this organization, would have been privy to the events transpiring in Dallas. In fact, he stated that he was called to the church because of the "scores of letters" he had written for R. C. Buckner, editor of the *Texas Baptist* and a participant in the controversy at First Dallas.[12] Thus, one may surmise that Hayden assumed the pastorate of the Live Oak congregation with his eyes wide open.

The schism at the First Baptist Church of Dallas had been caused by the acceptance of John Bodkin Link, the editor of the *Texas Baptist Herald* since 1865, into the church membership during a Wednesday night prayer meeting on June 5, 1878.[13] Robert Cooke Buckner, then rival editor of the *Texas Baptist,* immediately appealed his admittance, based upon ordinance number ten of the First Baptist Church's Rules of Order. This provision disallowed the acceptance of a new member when there was known to be a valid objection by a member in good standing. Upon the occurrence of such an event, the matter was to be settled at a regular conference or business meeting. Several of the members who were in favor of accepting Link as a member believed that some official business did transpire during this prayer meeting. A future land transaction supposedly was briefly discussed and then tabled. The official *Minutes* of the church show some business, though minor, did occur. An official business meeting, however, was not formally called into session. Subsequent church *Minutes* demonstrate that the normal practice was to call business meetings into session. So, normal protocol obviously had not been followed. Whatever the case may have been, Buckner was not present at the prayer meeting, but his opposition to Link's admittance was well known.[14] For this reason, Buckner believed that he was well within his rights to disagree with this overt breach of church order.

The events that transpired during this prayer meeting do not appear to have occurred in good faith. The pastor, James Hudson Curry, knew of Buckner's objection before the meeting, but still wanted Link to join his congregation.[15] There is no stated reason as to why Curry breached normal protocol. The answer, however, becomes obvious when one examines the complex associational and geographical rivalries of the Baptists in Texas. Neither Curry[16] nor Link,[17] both affiliated with Dallas-based denominational concerns, favored the emerging denominational ascendency of the leaders of Waco University. The strong advocates of Waco University, part of the BGA, not only supported their school, but also wanted the denominational seat of power located in Waco. This became known as the "Waco Policy." Link disagreed with the Waco Policy, believing that a new centralized university should be built in another location that would consolidate Waco University with rival Baylor University.[18] One great university, he argued, would better serve Texas Baptists than two rival and mediocre schools. After the realignments of 1875, Link's newspaper was supporting the Baptist State Convention, the main rival of the Baptist General Association. Furthermore, since Dallas and Link's newspaper were deep within the traditional territorial boundaries of the BGA, Link would have been viewed by many BGA advocates, especially B. H. Carroll, the powerful pastor of the First Baptist Church of Waco, as an intruder.[19]

Curry opposed the Waco Policy for a different reason. In fact, he spoke out against the influence aggregated by Waco University and the BGA's newly acquired periodical, the *Texas Baptist,* at the 1879 regular session of the Baptist General Association. On this occasion Curry went so far as to offer a proposal that would move the BGA away from such close relationships. Although his motion was denied, the damage was done. By proposing this motion, Curry had not only spoken out against the Waco Policy, but had also publically aligned himself against his own congregant, R. C. Buckner, and a large number of BGA supporters who backed Waco's denominational lead. A plausible explanation for this is that Curry, hoping to block advancement of the Waco establishment, may have realized when Link came forward for membership in 1878 that he needed a statewide newspaper to back his cause. And it no doubt seemed prudent to Curry that like-minded editor Link should be admitted to the membership, since he was still the editor of the pro-BSC *Texas Baptist*. This stance would have caused him to be perceived as an intruder in pro-BGA Dallas. Curry's policy, while pro-Dallas, created a split between himself and Buckner that was in place prior to Hayden's arrival. For all intents and purposes, though Hayden was years removed from the scene, the Hayden Controversy was born from these early actions. The night of June 5, 1878, set in motion a spiraling chain of events that would last for the remainder of the century and beyond.

Despite the unusual state of affairs, Curry and the majority of the First Baptist congregation believed that Buckner would eventually accept Link's membership. However, rather than quietly acquiescing, many members agreed with Buckner and demanded that Link's membership be rescinded. For the next two months the situation significantly intensified as disgruntled members gossiped against each other in every venue of Dallas. Finally, it was determined that some type of official action must be taken lest the church's witness in the community be destroyed. After a church-wide vote on July 10, 1878, the discontented members were denied satisfaction by a forty-three to twenty-two count. But the reaffirmation of the membership of Link and his wife Ada failed to end the dispute. According to critics, a disgruntled Buckner and his backers would never let the situation rest. For the remainder of the year Link and Buckner traded letters in an apparent attempt to reconcile differences, but they were not conciliatory in nature and were often leaked to the public. Furthermore, both parties berated the other in their respective periodicals. The First Baptist Church's first official response to these events disclosed the displeasure of church leaders with Buckner, who "claimed to be the aggrieved party, but refused or failed to seek a private conference with Elder Link, as the scriptures require, and that he might ascertain whether his grievances were well or ill founded, but instead published them to the world, to the injury of Elder Link, and circulated them extensively to poison and prejudice the membership of this church."[20] As recorded in the official church *Minutes,* Buckner's opponents at First Baptist concluded that he was just a "cantankerous old fool."[21]

In an attempt to heal the widening breach, the deacon body proposed that the aggrieved parties appoint a committee to work out an amiable reconciliation. Aware that the majority of the committee was against him, Buckner officially refused the offer at a called church session on December 24. As Buckner saw the matter, had the committee rendered a verdict against him, the remainder of the church would have been privy only to the verdict and would never have heard his interpretation of the affair. Furthermore, Buckner remained convinced that Link had joined the church for no other reason than to generate a larger readership, damage his standing in Dallas, and undermine the BGA. in its own territory. Buckner made this clear in virtually every edition of the *Texas Baptist* from May until December of 1878. In response, Link hurled the charge back at Buckner, accusing him of the very offences he blamed on others. Since the committee had apparently been stacked in his favor, Link had no problem with allowing the committee to settle the affair. Until his dying days, Link continued to claim that he had moved to Dallas in order to help Dr. F. M. Law promote educational endeavors. Buckner and Link were both prideful and stubborn men, and neither was willing to back away. And in time the words became too bitter and the wounds too deep for reconciliation.

Soon after his arrival in Dallas, Hayden remarked that every member in the church had been forced to take sides in the affair, and the First Baptist Church was split between the "Link Party" and the "Buckner Party."[22] The fact that Buckner refused to participate in any restorative discussions surprised many members of First Baptist. In *Dallas Church Vindicated,* W. N. Griffeth stated: "No one probably supposed that Elder Buckner would or could refuse, or would avoid an effort to settle the difficulty or shrink from the fullest investigation, if it should come to that, after having said so much and claimed to have so many charges against Elder Link."[23] Since only about one-fifth of the church had adopted his decision and the committee was clearly against him, Buckner's participation in such an event would have been futile.

On December 24, 1879, rather than work through what he believed to be a biased committee, Buckner was finally able to tell his side of the story in a carefully crafted speech at the Wednesday night business meeting. Known as the *Memorial*, this harsh speech recounted several of Buckner's reasons for disapproving Link's membership and the corresponding action of Curry. Buckner argued that a church cannot "walk together" and function as a fellowship where there is no unanimity within the congregation. He stated that this was the reason Baptist churches insist on a consensus for the acceptance of a new member. Pastor Curry knew of the disapproval of several members, but chose to ignore it. And, when those who disapproved made their opinions officially known, Curry continued to disregard congregational unity.

Buckner also claimed that since he and his followers kept these principles, which were stated in the original church constitution, they were not in error. For these reasons, Buckner claimed that the minority that followed proper church polity and voted to rescind Link's membership was the true First Baptist Church of Dallas. Buckner's faction then broke fellowship with the majority that had sided with Curry and Link. Due to their acceptance of Buckner's *Memorial*, the fifty-nine members who signed the document became known as the "Memorialites."

After long deliberations, the First Baptist Church decided that Link had done everything that Scripture required to be received into full membership. It was even known that two of Buckner's allies who supposedly disliked Link were in attendance and voted for his admittance. Following this action, the First Baptist Church began to eliminate the Memorialites from the official membership. As the targeted ringleader of the troublesome minority, Buckner was ordered to turn in his ordination papers and ministerial licence. Buckner flatly refused to comply and began to serve as the official minister to his followers. Buckner and the disgruntled Memorialites would later form the core of the Live Oak Baptist Church in East Dallas in May 1880.

There has been some conjecture concerning the ecclesiology of the Live Oak Baptist Church. Because of the fact that James Robinson Graves, the father of Landmarkism, occasionally spoke at the church, together with the membership's belief in closed communion, the Memorialites have been characterized as firm advocates of Landmarkism, a specific set of church doctrines that existed only in certain Baptist churches. In particular, Landmarkist doctrine taught that the Baptist Church was the only true church, the one that served as God's visible kingdom on earth, practiced closed communion, and traced its lineage back in an unbroken line to John the Baptist. All other religious bodies were in error. Though very few churches maintain these beliefs in the twenty-first century, Landmarkism dominated much of Texas Baptist doctrine in the nineteenth century. The remnant at the First Baptist Church managed to escape this stigma because it did not maintain closed communion. The split, therefore, has been perceived as occurring along ecclesiological lines, but this is difficult to prove.

According to historian Karen Bullock, a leading R. C. Buckner scholar, Buckner, the father of the Memorialites, did not demonstrate any overt Landmark tendencies.[24] In fact, his father lost his pastorate in Somerset, Kentucky, because he was not an advocate of Landmarkism.[25] This misunderstanding may come from the fact that Buckner borrowed one of Graves's arguments when making his case in the *Memorial*. Buckner, as Graves had done during his dispute at the First Baptist Church of Nashville, claimed that in a church split the true congregation was the faction that upheld the principles outlined in the church constitution.[26] Though coined by the father of Landmarkism, this argument is not particularly Landmarkist. Dozens of Baptist churches have employed this argument in order to keep their church from being taken over by those who have moved away from the faith on which the church was founded. In fact, this argument is still applied in similar situations in the modern Baptist church.[27]

In addition, J. R. Graves was popular in Texas, as evidenced by the fact that his newspaper, *The Tennessee Baptist*, was held in high regard and read statewide.[28] Yet, because he spoke at the Live Oak Church rather than at the First Baptist Church, it has been speculated that this characterized it as a more Landmark church. As it turns out,

Graves was not nearly as particular about where he preached as one might think. In fact, he had even preached the convention sermon for the BSC in 1859, the association which typically demonstrated fewer overt Landmark tendencies than the BGA. No matter where Graves preached in Texas, he and his teachings were popular.

Moreover, though closed communion is a commonly perceived tenet of Landmarkism, the rationale as to why the Live Oak Baptist Church adopted this position was probably more of a statement to the remnant at the First Baptist Church than an espousal of ecclesiology (church doctrine). The adoption of closed communion by the Live Oak congregation may have been a reaction to the First Baptist Church's refusal to allow the Memorialites access to the building.[29] On more than one occasion Buckner's followers showed up at the church building to hold services but were denied access. They were perceived as troublemakers and believed to have been bent on the destruction of Pastor Curry. Since the Memorialites had been officially disfellowshiped from their old church, they may have adopted closed communion in order reciprocate the sentiment that their erring brethren were not welcome in their services either. This explanation would concur with Buckner's apparent lack of strong Landmark doctrine.

Furthermore, there is no mention within the *Minutes* of the First Baptist Church or any other primary source that would lead one to conclude that the split was based on a matter of ecclesiology. The Memorialites may have held to some general tenets of Landmarkism, as did many prominent Texas Baptists like B. H. Carroll, but the schismatic events in Dallas were not primarily due to doctrine. This split was based on denominational alignments, associational rivalries, newspaper jealousies, and the haughtiness of their respective leaders.

Despite the personal nature of this conflict, the affair at the First Baptist Church of Dallas was a local version of the larger events that were unfolding between the two leading Texas Baptist conventions.[30] From the advent of the BGA in 1855, under the name East Baptist Convention, there had been a continued enmity between the two associations. In fact, the East Baptist Convention stated that its birth was due to BSC's failure to provide east Texas with appropriate mission funds.[31] The events taking place in Dallas were merely another chapter in this intense rivalry, and the combatants chose newspapers as their weapons. In this regard, Buckner's organ clearly supported Waco University and the General Association. Link's periodical had recently begun to support Baylor University and the State Convention. Though these newspapers were independently owned and received no official financial support from either convention, the editors of these papers were fierce warriors for their respective movements and thus each held the other and his adopted organization in an unfavorable light.

Despite their animosity, Buckner and Link had been acquaintances for many years. Moreover, the backgrounds of the men bore striking similarities. Both had attended Georgetown College in Kentucky, were zealous ministers, had a strong sense for business, and were fervent participants in Texas Baptist affairs. Nevertheless, an intense rivalry had begun to develop between them as early as 1875. The origin of the problem resonated from the Baptist General Association's official endorsement of Link's *Texas Baptist Herald*. Link was pleased with this honor, but a warning had been coupled with the endorsement. The foreboding statement declared: "We would impose no restrictions upon the independence of the press, but those who conduct them should be far from assuming a dictatorial spirit and striving to crush all who may have independence to differ with them."[32]

The addendum was due to Link's failure to give editorial support to the Waco Policy and the corresponding agenda of Waco University president, R. C. Burleson. This resolution made the terms of the fragile relationship between the editor and the BGA clear. The *Texas Baptist Herald* would remain the organ of the General Association if Link would support Burleson and his anti-centralization program. This would prove to be difficult since Link strongly opposed Burleson on this position. This difference of opinion would drive a wedge between these two powerful men until final consolidation took place in 1886.

It is important to note that during this period Waco University and the BGA were thriving, while Baylor University and the BSC were suffering a period of economic and numerical decline. The strongest Baptist presence in Texas was clearly in the north and east as new settlers continued to pour into these regions.[33]

The advocates of the Waco Policy wanted their university to remain intact and under BGA direction.[34] Thus, centralization may not have been an attractive option for the Waco constituents. Due to their recent success, those in favor of the Waco Policy may have believed that Waco University and the BGA could not only survive this period, but also continue to thrive without consolidation. One of the primary reasons that Waco University was dominating the Texas Baptist educational situation was President Burleson's sudden change of allegiance. In 1861 Burleson had resigned his post as president of Baylor University at Independence and accepted the presidency of Waco University. To make matters worse, he brought the entire faculty and senior class with him to Waco. Burleson carried a grudge against the trustees of Baylor at Independence because they did not allow him to have full control of the women's program. This personal hostility undergirded Burleson's efforts to destroy Baylor at Independence and the Baptist State Convention.

The strength of those in favor of the Waco Policy was further bolstered by the fact that Baptists moving to Texas were settling primarily in the BGA territories of north and central Texas. J. M Dawson, a prominent Baptist pastor and historian, estimated that there were as many as 50,000 Baptists in this region during this period.[35] Furthermore, Baptists who lived in the southern regions of Texas were migrating away from traditional BSC territory. A prime example may be noted in the decrease of membership of the Union Association, the home of Baylor University. In 1880 the association reported more than 3,000 members, but in 1883 the number had dropped to 1,803.[36] The growth of Washington County itself, which was the home of Independence and Baylor University, had also become stagnant. In 1880 Washington County reported a population of 27,565, but in 1887 the citizenry had grown to only 30,851. In addition, in 1887 the population of Independence was only 400.[37] The Elm Fork Association, which in 1903 would become the Dallas Baptist Association, however, was experiencing a period of unprecedented growth. In 1880 the Elm Fork Association had 1,155 members. In 1885 the membership numbered 2,196.[38] Dallas County had also experienced substantial growth, reporting in 1880 a population of 33,488. By 1887 the populace had grown to 77,323. Furthermore, McLennan County, the home of Waco University, had witnessed dramatic growth. In 1880 the county had a population of 26,934, but by 1887 the number had grown to 38,001.[39] The Waco Association had also grown during this period. In 1881 it reported 2,049 members. Six years later it had 2,693.[40] The population of Waco itself had grown during this period from 7,295 to 18,000.[41] Demographics such as these explain why Texas Baptist historian L. R. Elliott stated that the advocates of the Waco Policy were gaining ground. "Under this situation," stated Elliott, "Baylor University at Independence, with William Carey Crane as president, waxed weaker and weaker, while Waco University, with R. C. Burleson as president, waxed stronger and stronger."[42] Clearly Burleson and Waco University represented the future of Texas Baptists.

Despite Baylor's weakened situation, President William Carey Crane was against consolidation. Aside from institutional pride,[43] Crane shouldered the sentiment of Baylor alumni, "who heard in it [consolidation] the death knell of their locality as the abiding place of their institutions."[44] Crane's staunch attitude had been passed on to many of his former students, many of whom would have preferred to see Baylor pass out of existence rather than consolidate at Waco.[45]A prime example was Baylor trustee Harry Haynes, who was dead set "against the removal of the university" under any circumstance. But most Baylor men, such as Dr. William Howard, preferred life in Waco to death in Independence, recognizing that Baylor University was not as economically secure as Waco University. Enrollment numbers attest to this. In 1875 Baylor had only 75 students[46] and by 1885 only 28.[47] Waco University, however, enrolled more than 250 students in 1875[48] and more than 300 in 1885.[49] Thus, Waco University and its BGA advocates held several advantages over their rivals to the south.

Link's editorial acquiescence to the Waco mandates, however, was not to be. A few months after Link had received his ultimatum at the 1873 regular session of the BGA, he again began to push for educational consolidation within the pages of the August 21, 1873, edition of the *Texas Baptist Herald*. In virtually every edition Link attempted to stir interest for one Baptist university. On May 13, 1875, he made yet another dramatic plea for centralization. After this editorial outburst, the standing of the Baptist newspapers was reversed by the Waco advocates and president Burleson at the regular session of the General Association at Sherman in 1875. For Burleson, centralization at the cost of the Waco Policy was unthinkable. Buckner, however, had gained editorial favor by vowing to support the premises of the Waco Policy.[50] At this point, it was decided that Buckner's paper was now the "best medium of communication among the brethren of the General Association." Despite this, Link still felt that centralization of the Baptist universities remained the only viable option for a quality education. After the occurrence of these events, Link came to believe that Burleson was trying to crush both him and his newspaper due to his continued opposition.

Meanwhile, the situation at the First Baptist Church of Dallas worsened in 1880. Since the Memorialites continued to claim to be the genuine First Baptist Church of Dallas, a quandary developed over who should be seated as the true messengers of the church at the regular sessions of the BGA. A Called Session of the BGA met at the First Baptist Church of Dallas on February 24, 1880, in order to clarify the problem. Despite his known distaste for Link, R. C. Burleson was elected moderator of the affair, and an investigative committee was instructed to examine all the available written information.[51]

Although many members of both factions were present, very few oral testimonies were solicited. In fact, Link claimed in the March 4, 1880, edition of the *Texas Baptist Herald* that Pastor Curry was not even allowed to speak. Indeed, Curry had not been allowed to testify because the committee determined that only members in good standing in their church could be official messengers and thus recognized to speak. According to the committee, the Buckner faction had followed Baptist polity and was in good standing, while the Link-Curry party had not. Since the clerk of the church had sided with the Memorialites and his notes were perceived to be slanted in their favor, the Link-Curry group felt a desperate need for verbal testimony to buoy its case. On several occasions Link attempted to voice his opinion, but was ruled out of order by either Burleson or B. H. Carroll, members of the committee.[52]

During the ordeal it became apparent that Carroll was openly siding with the Buckner faction. J. B. Cranfill confirmed this, asserting that Carroll had played a masterful role during the hearings.[53] That should come as no surprise since the two men had been carrying out something of a theological feud in the pages of the *Texas Baptist Herald* for some time, and as of August 1877 Carroll had been listed as the associate editor of Buckner's newspaper. Link had accused the mighty Carroll of maintaining a works-based faith and as such not being a true Baptist. As the situation became more and more agitated, these powerful Texas Baptists grew to despise each other.

The problem faced by the Link-Curry faction was deepened by the fact that Buckner, a key participant in the charges against this faction, was also a member of the BGA Board of Directors. Link believed that Buckner's friends did everything within their power to keep the truth about the situation hidden. He suggested that the trial was designed to validate Buckner and castigate Link before the whole state. To this effect, Link stated in the March 4, 1880, edition of the *Texas Baptist Herald*: "there is not a man in Texas guilty of any crime who could be convicted where the judge, jury, evidence and solicitors were all of his own selecting, and no one permitted to offer a witness or say a word in opposition to the accused." Ironically, this encounter was reminiscent of the way Buckner had been treated the previous December when Curry attempted to fill the peace committee with his own advocates. Only this time it was Curry who was at a disadvantage. Curry's perceived inability to deal with the matter within the church in an evenhanded manner had forced the Buckner faction to take its case to the next level. By rendering this verdict, the BGA committee had demonstrated its disapproval of Curry's handling of the Link affair and its desire to win the debate at any ecclesiological cost.

The outcome, however, may have been sealed at an earlier date. Curry's disastrous attempt at reform during the 1879 regular session of the BGA and the perceived mistreatment of Buckner would not be forgotten by the advocates of the Waco Policy. By speaking out against the Waco Policy, Curry started the process that would secure his church's fate at this meeting the ensuing year. Because Buckner's faction remained true to the stated principles of the church, the committee found in favor of the Memorialites and they were recognized as the legitimate representatives of the First Baptist Church of Dallas.

In an interesting twist, Dr. I. M. Kimbrough (1826–1902), who had brought the morning sermon and was not a member of either church, was given the floor to address the assembly. Almost as a precursor to future Baptist battles, Kimbrough stated:

> Great Baptist principles were involved that could not be discussed in five minutes. He said that he was not partial to either side. The Association had no ecclesiastical existence and it had no right to interfere in the matters of a church, which recognized no higher power than itself to its own troubles .The Baptist denomination would not recognize the right of that body to settle a church difficulty.[54]

The importance of Kimbrough's statement did not escape Link. He clearly understood Kimbrough as saying that this action would "erect the General Association into a judicature higher than a sovereign, independent church, and that this was contrary to the New Testament."[55] This statement was made in defense of a very important Baptist principle: the autonomy of the local church. B. H. Carroll responded to Kimbrough, declaring that the committee was merely making a decision in reference to which faction was the true church and thus entitled to membership in the Baptist General Association. Since Kimbrough had not contributed a better idea, the deliberations of the committee would stand. Carroll's reaction to Kimbrough is somewhat puzzling, considering his own stated belief in the autonomy of the local church and his hatred of episcopal organizations.[56] Said Carroll in *Christ and His Church*: "The Church is a Divine institution. It is the only visible religious organization that is of a specific Divine Appointment."[57] Therefore, Carroll's response seems to buttress the notion that the immediate matter at hand was not ecclesiology, but rather an attempt to ensure a victory for the Buckner faction of the First Baptist Church. This would not be the last time that Carroll would set aside his own doctrinal beliefs in order to acquire a personal victory.

A similar sovereign church argument would be employed by S. A. Hayden during the height of his agitations in the 1890s. In this regard, Link himself must shoulder the majority of the blame for bringing this argument to light. In order to demonstrate how his faction was being overrun by the BGA forces, Link published Kimbrough's speech in the *Texas Baptist Herald*.[58] As a prominent member of the BGA, Hayden would have certainly read this article and would not have failed to recognize the strength of its arguments.

This February 1880 called session was a harbinger to the demise of the First Baptist Church of Dallas's standing within the ranks of the Baptist General Association.[59] These events forced Pastor Curry to realize that he and the First Baptist Church of Dallas, even if they managed eventually to regain their messenger status, would never be looked upon as leaders in the BGA. By September of the following year the First Baptist Church of Dallas elected representatives to attend the meeting of their former rival, the Baptist State Convention. With this action, the *Texas Baptist Herald* found a fresh audience in the membership of its new affiliation. Furthermore, each group now had a newspaper that was staged to enhance its own position and ferociously attack the convictions of the other. The events of the First Baptist Church of Dallas, therefore, created a ripple effect that was leading to a growing statewide condition of rivalry, anxiety, and distrust.

Realizing that they would never acquire the church building, the Memorialites purchased a piece of land on Live Oak Street.[60] They joined the Elm Fork Baptist Association and by May 1881 reported more than 200 members.[61] Prior to the arrival of Hayden in 1883, Buckner, W. H. Parks, who would become a strong Haydenite, and G. W. Pickett pastored the Live Oak Church. At the Elm Fork Associational meeting of 1881 the Memorialites were first recognized as the First Baptist Church meeting at Live Oak Street. With the completion of their church building in 1882, the Memorialites sent a conciliatory letter to the First Baptist Church on August 6, 1882, in hopes of restoring peace between the congregations. But the wounds were too fresh and the letter was rejected. Despite the fact that the Memorialites were the schismatic group, it should be noted that they appeared to be the more conciliatory faction.

This was the bitter situation that greeted S. A. Hayden when he assumed the Live Oak pastorate, or as he called it, the "Buckner Baptist Church," in April of 1883. Interestingly, Hayden stated that before he could accept the embattled pastorate, the church must officially adopt the name Live Oak Baptist Church and cease calling itself the First Baptist Church meeting at Live Oak Street. He did not believe the congregation had an authentic claim to this title.[62] This indicates that Hayden rejected Buckner's claim that his faction was the true First Baptist Church based on the "foundational purposes" voiced in the *Memorial.* Whether a cardinal element of Landmarkism or not, J. R. Graves was the architect of this defense, and Hayden's actions demonstrated his rejection of its premise.

With Hayden's arrival in Dallas reconciliation moved quickly. After only a month he came to the realization that the city could neither spiritually nor denominationally support two Baptist churches. In regards to each other, the two churches were certainly not acting in a Christian manner. Each group started rumors against the other, their respective members refused to do business with each other, and both sides were seriously damaging any chance of growth for the Baptist denomination in Dallas County.

In an attempt to begin the healing process, the First Baptist Church's new pastor, Robert Taylor Hanks, instigated several meetings to explore the possibility of reconciliation with Pastor Hayden. This move toward peace and reunification had been strengthened by the resignation of Pastor Curry, whose lack of strong pastoral skills and personal ambition had escalated the split.[63] It was also well known that several members of the First Baptist Church who had not fled to the Live Oak Church believed Curry was ministering only to a faction of the church.[64] At any rate, the new pastors agreed to quell the disruptive quarrels they had inherited. Although the budding friendship was short lived, their initial meetings were cordial. First Baptist Church of Dallas remained in fellowship with the BSC and the Live Oak Church remained affiliated with the BGA.

At this point the original leader of the insurrection, R. C. Buckner, took the lead in the healing process. In April of 1883 he proposed that the congregants meeting at Live Oak withdraw their *Memorial* and drop their claim to being the true First Baptist Church of Dallas. These acts of goodwill were instrumental to breaking the stalemate between the rival congregations. Once the *Memorial* was retracted, Buckner made a stirring speech begging for reconciliation so that the Baptist cause in Texas might escape further damage. "Can we not do this in the interest of conciliation and peace?" asked Buckner, adding:

> I know your spirit and believe you will answer, Yes. What does the paper before us propose to rescind. The Memorial referred to, and such acts following it as affect the relations of the two bodies and individual members of the same. These are not essential to the perpetuity of the church and we can well afford, under the shadow of the cross and in the interest of the subject sought, to rescind them.[65]

Steps toward reconciliation now moved more rapidly. On May 6, 1883, Pastor Hayden read a response from the First Baptist Church of Dallas to the Live Oak congregants that spelled out a willingness to reconcile. A resolution was then adopted that accepted their offer for peace. On June 3, 1883, the two churches held a unified service: Pastor Hayden presided and Pastor Hanks delivered the message. Over the next year good will between the congregations improved significantly. So much progress was made that both churches believed a formal reconciliation was imminent. Therefore, on March 30, 1884, the Live Oak Church and the First Baptist Church of Dallas held another joint service. Within a year the reconciliation was complete.

The plans for reconciliation were carefully drawn. No one wanted another outbreak of hostility. It was decided that Hanks, not Hayden, would be pastor of the unified church. This choice came about as the result of a "silent vote," which apparently was unanimous.[66] This turn of events raises important questions. Why was Hanks selected over Hayden? And how, with all the previous troubles, could it have been a unanimous vote? The answer may be found in denominational politics.

In June 1883 Hayden purchased the *Texas Baptist* from Buckner. A short time afterward he stepped down as the full-time pastor of the Live Oak Church and Buckner took the lead. Hayden continued to take a ministerial role at the church, but not on a full-time basis. This action appears to indicate that he was more interested in being editor of his new periodical than pastor of First Baptist Church of Dallas. Thus, the vote to elect Hanks was unanimous because Hayden made the motion that Hanks assume the pastorate.[67] Hayden, however, remained one of the more influential members of the First Baptist Church of Dallas and continued to perform miscellaneous ministerial roles for the congregation. In particular, he still officiated at many church weddings and funerals. Even though he was not the official pastor, Hayden's actions demonstrated his desire for everyone in the church to know he was the true shepherd of the church.

Reunification notwithstanding, many of the denominational allegiances that had fostered the initial split still existed. Even though the Live Oak Church and the First Baptist Church were again one body, the Live Oak faction remained loyal to the BGA, while the First Baptist Church group continued its firm support of the BSC.[68] In fact, Pastor Hanks, a BSC advocate, became fast friends with Link and openly endorsed the *Texas Baptist Herald*. This appears to have raised the ire of the new editor of the *Texas Baptist*. Realizing the complexity of the situation, Hanks stated that he fancied himself "as the pastor of a double-barreled church." For this reason, the First Baptist Church sent messengers to both the BGA and the BSC. It was not uncommon for a church to send visiting messengers to an association with which it was not affiliated, but these were official messengers. So the church was still divided, and Hanks was having difficulty maintaining the peace. Link stated that if it were not for the overwhelming popularity of Pastor Hanks, the rancor that ensued would have been enough to warrant his dismissal. Over the next two years the tension and animosity between Hanks and Hayden continued to grow. Though their disagreement had initially developed over convention loyalty and newspaper support, by 1888 it had become a personal matter. Due to his initial disregard of Hayden and his newspaper, Hanks would be forced to bear the brunt of several unfounded rumors, many of which later would be proven to have originated in Hayden's harangues.

Despite the obvious potential for a schism, Hayden was one of the key mitigators in the reconciliation of the First Baptist Church of Dallas. That Hayden chose to come to Dallas and to assume the pastorate of the Live Oak Church during its most trying years cannot be overlooked. Hayden was clearly a peacemaker; yet he made certain choices and geographic moves that suggest he may have wanted to be more prominent in Baptist affairs statewide, and the vehicle he chose was the press.

Hayden had been a witness to the power of the press in Texas Baptist matters. As editors of weekly Baptist papers, Link and Buckner were able to broadcast their opinions to large audiences, thereby attracting loyal followers across the state. It appears that Hayden wished to become an editor for similar reasons. As a consequence, he bought the *Texas Baptist* and stepped down from the Live Oak pulpit.

CHAPTER 2

An Unhappy Marriage

RECONSTRUCTION HAD BEEN DIFFICULT in Texas. Even though the state had been largely spared the scarred images of battlefields, the economy was in ruins. The financial problems that devastated the entire country had their roots in the overexpansion of the railroads. After the Civil War, the railroad added some 33,000 miles of track and employed tens of thousands of workers. A problem, however, occurred in 1873. Because it was unable to market the bonds for the Northern Pacific Railroad, the Banking House of Jay Cooke and Company had failed in early 1873. The failure of the Northern Pacific was a major factor in bringing on the Panic of 1873. Industries that depended on the railroad for cheap transportation feared they could not get their goods to market. Industries such as steel and cotton were forced to lay off thousands of workers and close hundreds of plants. By 1878 more than 10,000 companies had failed.[1]

Texas, too, experienced hard times, as jobs were lost and the price of cotton and other agrarian staples plummeted. This deep economic depression affected everyone, including the state's Baptists. Texas Baptists had too many organizations that required financial support. Clearly, there was a need for some retrenchment and reorganization.

Baptist Consolidation and Hayden's Victory

While the two First Baptist Churches of Dallas were trying to reconcile, the two rival state conventions were also attempting to consolidate.[2] However, the rivalries were still too strong to allow such an event to occur. The most significant obstacle to unification remained the Baptist university debate. Significant efforts at consolidation had been made at a joint BSC-BGA meeting in Bremond in 1875, but jealousies and reciprocal suspicions soon wrecked this effort.[3] In particular, the BSC believed that the BGA was merely trying to make Waco the educational and denominational center of Texas.[4] New problems began to emerge in 1882. Baylor University at Independence had always been affiliated with the BSC, its parent convention. In 1882 the BGA formally identified itself with Waco University.[5] Each organization now had its own official university. The repeated efforts of Link notwithstanding, it appeared that consolidation would never happen.

However, in 1883, under the leadership of B. H. Carroll, Hanks, and Hayden, significant strides were made in favor of consolidation.[6] At that year's BGA associational meeting in Cleburne, Carroll chaired a committee that took the first step toward the unification process. After meeting with the committee, Carroll made a stirring speech to the BGA representatives in which he implored them to work together with the other Texas Baptist bodies. He claimed that the rivalries and overlapping ministries of the various conventions had hampered the mission effort in Texas. The committee then voted to send a letter to the other four Texas conventions to demonstrate its desire for consolidation. In the letter Carroll was instructed to ask the other conventions three important questions concerning unification:

1. Is it desirable and expedient?
2. Is it practicable?
3. If so, under what form?[7]

Even though formal action was not undertaken by the BGA messengers at that time, the line of communication had been opened.[8] In fact, the BSC failed to officially acknowledge the reception of this message.[9] The BSC appeared to be less receptive to any discussion concerning consolidation. Of this initial gesture Baylor University president William Carey Crane suggested, "The plums were too green then to be gathered." At this point in the educational ordeal Crane may have been the BSC's strongest opponent of consolidation. He had poured his life, money, and energies into Baylor University at Independence and feared that consolidation would spell the school's demise.

Since the BSC had failed to embrace this initial offer, the BGA also took the second step in the consolidation process at its regular session in Ennis in 1885. Several resolutions were tendered, but the most significant and strongest call for centralization of the universities and consolidation of the conventions was made by Hayden, who stated:

> Whereas, the Baptists of Texas, led, as we believe, by the Spirit of God, are seeking some practical basis of fraternal union, and,
> Whereas, we believe the prayer of Christ, that His people, "might all be one" is destined to a complete fulfillment, and,
> Whereas, institutions of learning are powerful agencies for good or evil, as they are directed by Christian or anti-Christian influences, and,
> Whereas, we can only hope to educate our youth by providing facilities for attaining knowledge equal to the secular institutions of the country, and
> Whereas, the securement of the perfect accord our people in Texas centers largely upon our denominational interests, therefore resolved,
> 1. That in order to remove any obstacles that may be in the way of our future concert of action in advancing the Baptist cause in Texas, it is, in our judgement, desirable, that all our denominational institutions of learning in Texas be united into one Baptist State University.

> 2. That we, the Baptist General Association of Texas, pledge ourselves to meet any proposition looking to such consolidation of schools upon principles of fairness and equality.
> 3. We believe that we do but express the sentiment of the great Baptist family of Texas, as well as provide for the best interests of the proposed consolidated in making it a condition of such consolidation that Rufus C. Burleson, D. D., L. L., the only survivor of the great men who have laid the foundation of Baptist education in Texas, and who has spent his entire life in that work, be made the chancellor for life of the said consolidated university, with adequate salary.[10]

This passage is significant for several reasons. One can clearly determine that Hayden was not only a proponent of the consolidation of the universities, but he also "did more than his share" to promote a denominational conglomeration.[11] That Hayden wanted Burleson to be named president of the unified school is apparent in this resolution, and from this point forward he used his periodical to promote the Waco educator. Burleson, in turn, would play a significant role in many of Hayden's future endeavors. Furthermore, those who seconded this resolution must have realized the exigency of immediate action. It was well known that as long as the current presidents of Baylor and Waco universities were alive, consolidation could never occur.[12] On February 27, 1885, Crane died. This provided the opportunity for the advocates of the Waco Policy to secure not only the location of the university, but also to recommend a new president. In an attempt to make the offer of consolidation more conciliatory and less threatening, Hanks wanted it made clear that this was not an attempt to usurp BSC authority. The motion was accepted. Though not mentioned in the resolution, it was known that the university question was the most significant obstacle in the unification of the Baptist conventions. If the universities joined, the various conventions and their satellite organizations could follow suit.

It was now time for the BSC to make a decision. The advocates of the BSC realized that their school and convention were both declining in numbers. The northward migration of Baptists out of traditional BSC territory into BGA areas had continued. Baylor University could no longer even afford to pay its professors.[13] The solid leadership of Crane was no longer present. When the BSC leadership looked northward, it saw that the BGA and Waco University were thriving. The numbers did not lie. Waco University enrolled more than 300 students in 1885, while Baylor University enrolled only 75. Furthermore, the numerical and fiscal success of the schools' parent conventions mirrored that of the universities. On the one hand, in 1885 the BGA reported that it had organized 51 churches and 89 Sunday Schools. On the other hand, the BSC had organized only 19 churches, though both had baptized almost the same number of people. A contemporary historian stated that "they were both great reports, with the advantage in favor of the General Association."[14]

The strengths and weaknesses of the two conventions were echoed in their leadership. The great Baptist figures of this period, such as B. H. Carroll, R. C. Buckner, R. C. Burleson, J. M. Carroll, and S. A. Hayden, were all BGA constituents. With the deaths of R. E. B. Baylor and W. C. Crane the BSC had lost its strongest supporters.[15] With the inevitable at hand, during the 1885 regular session of the BSC at Lampasas, a joint BSC and BGA committee met to discuss the feasibility of the merger. A. W. Dunn reported: "Your committee on consolidation of education interests of the Baptists of Texas beg leave to report that it is the sense of this Convention that the consolidation of our institutes of learning is desirable."[16] A resolution adopting this statement quickly followed. It was decided that representatives of the BSC and the BGA would meet in Temple on December 9, 1885, in order to work out the details of the unification.[17]

The Temple meeting was very significant in the unification process. Hanks was the logical choice for moderator, due to the unique dual associational alignment of his church, and he took the lead. The proceedings were cordial but did not unfold smoothly. Over the years people had expended a great amount of money, time, and energy in an attempt to save their respective conventions and universities, and now consolidation was about to occur. J. M. Carroll reported: "Few, if any, secured all they wanted, and some secured probably nothing as they really wanted it."[18] Yet, the consolidation of both the Baptist universities and conventions managed to move forward.

Each body appointed five men to a committee that would outline the details of the universities' merger. On the morning of December 11, 1885, the chairmen of the committee, B. H. Carroll and C. R. Breedlove, presented the resolution. The most important aspects included:

> 1. That Waco and Baylor Universities be consolidated.
> 2. The name of the school shall be Baylor University.
> 3. That Baylor University shall be located at Waco.[19]

After the consolidation of the universities had been accepted, the unification of the general bodies was less tumultuous. Though the BGA and the BSC were the strongest conventions in Texas, they had not been the only statewide organizations in Texas. In fact, there had been at least another three smaller conventions located throughout the state. These entities, however, had been brought into the fold of the BSC. The Northern Baptist Convention reentered in 1883 and the Central and East Texas Conventions in 1884. Though no specific reason is given, geography appeared to be the determining factor in their decision. These smaller conventions were dispersed all over the state and the BGA held sway only in east Texas. Though the BSC's strongest influence was along the Gulf Coast, it still had advocates more widely dispersed across the state. It could not have been a financial decision. Both the BGA and BSC were tight with their money, especially if it concerned its dissemination to distant churches.

With this educational obstacle behind them, G. W. Smith was elected chairman of the committee, and he presented the following resolutions, which were adopted:

> 1. That the Baptist General Association of Texas be consolidated with the Baptist State Convention of Texas.
> 2. That the name of the consolidated body shall be "The Baptist General Convention of Texas."
> 3. That the basis of representation in the first meeting of the

> consolidated body shall be the same as heretofore . . .
> 4. That the mission work be continued until the first meeting as heretofore under the direction of the two general bodies respectively, and be supported until that meeting.
> 5. That the first meeting of the consolidated body be held at Waco, beginning on Tuesday after the first Sunday in July, 1886.[20]

Following the adoption of this resolution, Hayden brought forth another resolution, which was accepted. In the tone of an objective peacemaker, Hayden stated: "Resolved, that the phraseology used in the consolidation of the general bodies was an accommodation to the legal status of affairs and not in any sense to be construed as an invasion of the equality of the two bodies entering into the consolidation."[21]

Inasmuch as the unified university was to be located at Waco and presided over by R. C. Burleson, the offices of the BGCT were to be located in Waco, and the first unified convention was to be held at Waco, the advocates of the BSC must have felt somewhat dejected and slighted.[22] Perhaps sensing this unhappiness, Hayden, by making the aforementioned statement, let those who perhaps felt as if they had been disregarded know that he would treat them fairly and that they had a friend in the editor of the *Texas Baptist*. With this statement Hayden harkened back to his first edition of the *Texas Baptist* on July 15, 1883, when he stated: "We propose to be a faithful friend of every Baptist in the state." Hayden's conciliatory gesture and friendly embrace may have aided his standing before the body in the not so distant future.

With the conclusion of the Temple meeting, one must observe that in the first three years that Hayden had lived in Dallas he had not only helped reconcile the squabbling factions of the First Baptist Church of Dallas, but had also been an important contributor to the unification of the Baptist universities and the general bodies. Even Texas' most famous pastor, Z. N. (Wildcat) Morrell, believed editor Hayden was a unifier. In *Flowers and Fruits In the Wilderness,* he observed that since Hayden had "bought the *Texas Baptist* from Dr. Buckner in 1883, its policy has been to unite the Baptists of Texas. This has been done through it as the chief instrumentality."[23]

Two of three sources of contention had been resolved at Temple, but the third remained unsolved. Texas Baptists realized that a complete consolidation of denominational affairs also meant a consolidation of the newspapers. The problem was that both newspapers were privately owned by strong-willed men who did not want to give up their voice in Texas Baptist affairs. In the *Texas Baptist Herald* of December 24, 1885, Link went so far as to state: "we say now that Dr. Hayden's ideas and methods, and his way of looking at questions involved in almost every step in such an enterprise, are so diverse from ours, that we are unwilling to risk the consequences of consolidation with him."

Despite such misgivings, fellow churchmen met and corresponded for over a year in the hopes of arriving at a mutual agreement concerning the newspapers. At one point Link actually proposed that both men sell their papers to a third party that would work closely with the new convention. Hayden would hear nothing of it.[24] Each man wanted to be the editor and no middle ground could be reached.[25] Texas Baptists, however, wanted but one paper to complete the great unification process. In an attempt to cool the growing rhetoric, on January 14, 1886, Link wrote: "We have no doubt that consolidation of the papers will be effected very soon, and we trust wisely." After a year of futile attempts, the first annual session of the Baptist General Convention of Texas was called to order in Waco in July of 1886.

Unification of the Baptist newspapers was a popular topic of discussion by the messengers at this first annual session of the BGCT. Yet, nothing could be done because both newspapers were privately owned. Thus, the BGCT could not force the editors to consolidate, but only encourage them toward this hopeful end. In order to speed up the solution, a committee comprised of Link and Hayden advocates made a final attempt to resolve the impasse. This group concluded that for the good of the convention the papers must consolidate. Only one problem remained: location. The editor of the *Texas Baptist Herald*, even though his organ had traditionally been published at Austin, realized that in order to win the approval of the convention, Waco would have to be the new location. The editor of the *Texas Baptist*, however, wanted Dallas. Thus, it was clearly understood that the location of a unified periodical would determine which of these two men, Link or Hayden, would be editor. Once again the two most influential Baptist cities in Texas were at odds.

Hayden and Link agreed that the convention should decide the proper venue. Once more the Convention stated that it had no right to force its opinion on an independently owned newspaper. The Convention then abruptly adjourned, but the people did not leave their seats. It was decided that the messengers of the BGCT, while not in a regular session, could render an unofficial opinion.

After the official order of business had concluded, it was announced that Link and Hayden could unofficially address the messengers from the platform concerning the locale of the unified newspaper. This is the reason for the large vote. Everyone knew this pressing matter was about to be addressed. Hayden and Link agreed to accept the unofficial vote. Each editor spoke for almost twelve minutes in an attempt to rally support for his own city, either Dallas or Waco. This was the first time Hayden invoked Dallas sentiment to do battle against Waco interests, but it would not be the last. Even though the Convention was not in session, *Minutes* were kept and included in the official proceedings. The *Minutes* read:

> The order of business was suspended in order that S. A. Hayden might make some remarks on a question of privilege. The resolutions were presented:
>
> Whereas, all the great interests of Texas Baptists have been consolidated except their papers, viz: The Texas Baptist and The Texas Baptist and Herald, and
>
> Whereas, the editors of those two papers have agreed upon the complete basis of consolidation, except the place of location, and
>
> Whereas, they have jointly asked that the denomination say, so far as this Convention can utter the final voice of the denomination, what city we think the most desirable from which to publish—thereof,
>
> Resolved, that this body express its preference without discussion.[26]

Although no further discussion was to take place, B. H. Carroll, immediately prior to the vote, asked to address the messengers. With permission granted, he requested that the large Waco contingent recuse themselves from the vote. In turn, he surely hoped that the very large delegation from Dallas would do likewise.[27]

Hayden's later interpretation of these events discloses a conspiratorial frame of mind. Although they were BGA friends, Hayden believed Carroll's desire to have the unified paper in Waco overrode friendship. According to Hayden, Carroll was also willing to forget all the past problems that had taken place between himself and Link in the pages of the latter's newspaper. Though he did not immediately suspect an under-the-table deal, Hayden became convinced that Carroll had made a secret agreement with Link in order to secure a Waco victory. "Dr. Link should move his periodical to Waco in two weeks," Hayden stated. "Defendant Carroll was to keep this a secret . . . Defendant Carroll had accepted the statement confidentially, but on account of what Dr. Link had published about him previously 'he hated him as he hated a rattlesnake.'" Furthermore, Hayden claimed Link promised Carroll, in return for his aid in securing the unified periodical, never to print anything that would contradict the Waco pastor.[28]

Neither B. H. Carroll nor his multiple biographers have provided any information that would corroborate Hayden's story of intrigue. Carroll's record, however, demonstrated that several times throughout his career he could be manipulative and was not above back-room deals if he believed they might advance his goals. This assessment is documented in an article entitled "The Political Side of B. H. Carroll," by historian Glenn Jonas who demonstrated that Carroll could be extremely manipulative and often advocated issues that would advance his standing in the BGCT and the Southern Baptist Convention.[29] Carroll's most obvious case of manipulation took place in 1905 while he was the chairman of the board of trustees at Baylor University. At a regular board meeting in 1905 while Baylor president Samuel Palmer Brooks was in Europe, Carroll told the board that he had a vision of a great seminary in the Southwest that God wanted him to found. Obviously taken by the emotion of the moment and possibly intimidated by what might happen to them if they voted against Carroll, board members voted to separate the religion department from the rest of Baylor University. When Brooks returned home, he discovered that "one of his departments had become a separate institute."[30] In 1906, Baylor Theological Seminary was born and B. H. Carroll was its dean. Carroll, however, was not finished. He wanted the seminary to be relocated to another city so that his school would not be under the shadow of Baylor University. Carroll realized that President Brooks would never let this happen unless there was a tremendous groundswell of support from the Texas Baptist masses. In order to develop this groundswell, many of Carroll's friends, including James Franklyn Norris, began to promote Fort Worth as the natural location in many of the local papers. Before long Carroll had the support of the people and President Brooks caved in to Carroll. The seminary moved to Fort Worth in the fall of 1910.[31]

Given this pattern of behavior, it certainly appears that a behind-the-scenes deal to ensure the paper's location in Waco would not go against Carroll's ethics and personality. Carroll deemed the Waco Policy so important that he was willing not only to enlist his old rival Link, but also turn his back on his erstwhile friend Hayden. Carroll would allow nothing to stand in the way of his consolidation of power in Waco.

But the Dallas messengers put an end to any further Waco augmentation of power. Eager to have the paper in their city, the Dallas messengers failed to recuse themselves. They were determined to have at least one victory over their neighbor to the south. J. M. Carroll understood that this vote was viewed by the respective messengers as primarily a contest between Waco and Dallas.[32] Since the tally was so close, Dallas 169, Waco 168, a second vote was taken. This time the result was Dallas 177, Waco 174.

J. M. Carroll reported that "there were several messengers from the Waco First Baptist Church alone. If they had voted, the paper would have gone to Waco." The rivalry between the two cities and the excitement of the vote caused a tremendous amount of chaos on the floor. In fact, J. M. Carroll reported that a woman who had intended to vote for Waco got confused and accidently voted for Dallas. Nothing, however, ever came of this matter. To the chagrin of Carroll, the consolidated paper would be located in Dallas. Despite the obvious fact that Hayden was now the editor of the BGCT's sole organ, his paper was not subsequently endorsed by the messengers because the vote did not occur during an official session. The lack of official endorsement would prove to be pivotal in later developments.

In spite of the narrow vote, Hayden had won a decisive victory, and within an hour Link sold the *Baptist Herald* to Hayden for ten thousand dollars.[33] Link agreed to co-edit the periodical for a few months, but he realized his days as an editor had come to an end. Hayden wasted little time. He immediately consolidated the two papers, renamed the periodical the *Texas Baptist and Herald*, and promptly moved it to Dallas. Of course, this turn of events added fuel to the rivalry between Dallas and Waco, a rivalry that continued until 1896, when the BGCT offices were relocated to Dallas. This pleased the Dallas advocates and left Waco's supporters to content themselves with being the home of Baylor University. But even the university's location was not settled with finality until the 1920s, when the two Baptist cities engaged in another skirmish. As Dallas grew and Waco's populace remained dormant, several prominent Dallas Baptists attempted to relocate Baylor to Dallas. After a flurry of financial activity and controversy, the city of Waco pledged to raise a $1,000,000 endowment for Baylor if the university promised to remain in Waco permanently.[34] Baylor University accepted the offer and the rivalry between the two cities passed into memory. In the twenty-first century virtually no rivalry exists at all between Dallas and Waco.

Hayden now owned the only major Baptist periodical in Texas, and a great many people were pleased by this development. Texas Baptists were now unified as never before, and Hayden's voice and message would now carry considerable weight within the new BGCT. As of 1886 the Baptists of Texas could proudly boast of "one Baptist paper, one Baptist University, and but one general missionary body."[35]

CHAPTER 3

Bad Blood in Dallas Leads to Ill Will Across Texas

DURING THE 1880S, UNIFICATION was an important concept not only in the Baptist General Convention of Texas, but also in the many different areas of the secular world in Texas. The railroad in particular was a unifying force and Texas experienced significant growth in this industry. Prior to the Civil War there had been less than 500 miles of track in Texas. By 1890 there were 8,710 miles of track crisscrossing the Lone Star State connecting the smaller cities with the larger.[1] The development of the railroad shortened the great distances between cities and allowed all areas of the state to prosper financially. Perhaps nowhere in Texas did the railroad have a more positive financial impact than in the Baptist cities of Dallas and Waco.

The development of Dallas as a major city was closely tied to the development of the railroad. The Houston and Central Railroad opened a station in Dallas in July of 1872. The following year the Texas and Pacific Railroad set up operations. Just before the arrival of the Houston and Central, the population of Dallas was 1,200. In September 1873, just after the arrival of the Texas and Pacific, the population of Dallas soared to 7,000. In spite of the Panic of

1873, the railroad had made Dallas an important export center for cotton, grains, and other raw materials. The prosperity that came with the railroad led to the opening of new businesses and brought new advances like electricity and the telephone to the city. By 1890 Dallas was the largest city in Texas, with a population of 38,067.[2]

The railroad had also brought prosperity to the city of Waco. In the early 1880s the St. Louis and Southwestern railroads built stations in the city. Located in the center of the state, Waco became one of the most important gathering points of cotton from the surrounding region. Cotton would be shipped to Dallas and then exported out of the state to the rest of the world. The presence of the railroad and the corresponding boom in industry had led to an impressive growth in population. In 1870 the city's population was 749; in 1884, 12,000.[3]

The Opening Skirmishes

Unification of schools, conventions, and papers, notwithstanding, many unresolved problems remained for Texas Baptists, problems that would soon snap the fragile cord holding the infant BGCT together. No one more accurately described the destructive affairs that were about to unfold than J. M. Carroll: "We then—1886—had one Baptist paper, one Baptist University (Baylor College in addition), and but one general missionary body, not including the Sunday School and Colportage Convention. This condition lasted only two years as to a paper, only four years as to a school, and only fourteen years as to a general body."[4] Events during these years occurred simultaneously and at a furious pace.

As editor of the sole Baptist organ in Texas, Hayden probably expected to have an increased role in state-level decision making in the BGCT. He soon discovered this would not be the case. Despite his formidable newspaper presence, he began to realize that he would not be accepted as a charter member of the convention's developing power structure. The reasons were clear. If he had agreed to move his newspaper to Waco, he may have been soundly defeated by his popular statewide rival Link. Link's circulation list demonstrated that his following was statewide, while Hayden's seat of influence would always be in east Texas, and particularly Dallas. In fact, Dallas Baptist

Association historian Carl Suter claimed that "Hayden's influence in Dallas would become so strong that by 1899, 'he (Hayden) and his followers were in complete control of the association.'"[5] Hayden's popularity in this region was based on the perception that he was their voice and defender. In his bid to secure the denominational organ in Waco, B. H. Carroll had obviously sided against east Texas, Dallas, and Hayden. With these actions, the rivalry began to take on geographical aspects.

Due to B. H. Carroll's apparent efforts to secure the unified paper for Waco, many of Hayden's earliest writings suggest that Waco dominance was at the heart of the conflict.[6] This accusation would remain one of the staples of Hayden's complaints for the remainder of his journalistic career. Though sporadic and soft-spoken in tone, his articles began to hint that a small clique of powerful men sought dominance in all denominational matters. In particular, in the August 10, 1887, edition of his newspaper, Hayden informed the people of Texas that there was a "growing effort on the part of some men to impose their wills in disregard for unity." Due to the developing power of Waco, this barb was in all likelihood cast in their direction.

What Hayden did not print in his periodical was also significant. Unlike his predecessor Buckner, Hayden did not place news concerning Waco and the BGCT on the front page of his newspaper. These early incidents led several of the Baptist leaders to question Hayden's loyalty to the new BGCT. According to Texas Baptist historian L. R. Elliott, "From the time of consolidation in 1886, it became increasingly clear that S. A. Hayden could not bring himself to make the consolidated paper, which he now owned, an unreserved champion of the organized, cooperative mission work of Texas Baptists."[7] Similarly, J. B. Cranfill, hardly an unbiased observer, remarked: "All the time, however, an undercurrent of denominational sentiment was growing which was utterly opposed to Hayden and his methods."[8] These early salvos foreshadowed things to come, as old issues once again surfaced.

In spite of the best efforts by many, the reconciliation at the First Baptist Church of Dallas was never made complete. The earlier rivalry within the reunified church over convention alliances had been somewhat settled due to the advent of the BGCT, but Hanks neither reversed his earlier endorsement of Link's paper nor his continuing deprecation of Hayden's periodical.[9] Hayden viewed this lack of endorsement as a serious challenge to his potential convention leadership. His own pastor, the very same man for whom he had stepped aside in the First Baptist reunion, did not back his periodical. Therefore, their relationship was never more than cordial after 1885.[10] The words of Joseph Martin Dawson ring true: "there existed almost from the beginning of R. T. Hanks' pastorate of the First Church, Dallas, a conflict between him and S. A. Hayden, editor of the *Texas Baptist and Herald*."[11]

As early as 1887 rumors began to circulate throughout First Baptist Dallas that Pastor Hanks was "consorting with women in an unchristian manner."[12] The innuendo remained little more than an unproven murmur until September 9, 1888. At that point the deacon body of the First Church was forced to take official action. On November 18 the disputants were invited to make official charges before the church. Four complaints were presented to the congregation, three concerning Hanks' comportment with women, a fourth his conduct with former Live Oak Baptist Church pastor Hayden. In the years that followed, Hayden mentioned only the trouble Hanks had with various women, not with him.

The complaints were set forth by one of the original leaders in the Live Oak schism, W. H. Prather. The specific charges involving women were that Hanks visited a woman at the outskirts of town and went for long buggy rides with her on numerous occasions, "consorted" with a woman on a train bound for the Southern Baptist Convention in a manner that led at least one stranger to believe they were married, and perhaps the most serious, attempted "at various times during these past years. . . . to kiss and embrace young women, shocking their modesty and placing them in embarrassing situations." The last involved alleged "slanderous statements concerning S. A. Hayden . . . and at times cursing him."

A fourteen-person committee composed of members of the First Baptist Church as well as prominent outside ministers, such as B. H. Carroll, was to investigate these charges. Hayden apparently selected Carroll to be one of his representatives. Everyone in the church agreed to abide by the findings of the committee, whatever the result. In addition, no one was to speak a word of the matter until an official verdict had been rendered. After the verdict had been reached, each member in the church, as agreed upon at the original session, was instructed to sign a referendum verifying his or her agreement to let the matter pass into history.

Since rumors had grown at an alarming rate, the leadership of the First Baptist Church decided to head off as much potential trouble as possible. The Link-Buckner imbroglio had been unsettling enough, and no one wanted a repeat of that episode. So, even before the charges before Hanks were levied, the deacon body published a statement in the September 12 edition of Hayden's *Texas Baptist and Herald* claiming that "while we do not wish to forestall an investigation of the whole matter, yet we feel that the time has come and it is incumbent upon this church to speak out upon this subject, and extend to our pastor that support and comfort due from a church to its pastor."

In spite of the best intentions, the deacon body actually exacerbated the situation by this public announcement. Until then the alleged antics of Pastor Hanks had been relatively confined to local comments and unspecified innuendos within the congregation. The troublesome matters were now broadcast statewide and brought to the attention of a larger body of Baptists. Everyone who read the *Texas Baptist and Herald* realized that a new situation was brewing at the First Baptist Church of Dallas. To many outsiders this must have appeared as just another First Church squabble. After all, the Buckner-Link affair had been published extensively. As the situation intensified, Hayden's motive became suspect. It seemed the editor was all too eager to publish anything damaging to the man who had failed to stand in support of his newspaper concern.[13]

After a long period of intensive investigation and deliberation, the committee reached a decision, and a church-wide meeting was scheduled for December 14 to announce the results. All fourteen members apparently exonerated Hanks, an amazing verdict given the virulent nature of the conflict. This acquittal was also somewhat puzzling. How could these people arrive at a unanimous statement of innocence? An exact answer to this question cannot be offered; however, several of the peripheral events and comments that surrounded the deliberations help clarify the verdict.

The exoneration was coupled with a qualification: "[T]here have been certain improprieties of conduct which, while not assailing the moral purity of Mr. Hanks, yet in our judgement, were characterized by injudiciousness." This statement casts doubt on the decision of innocence rendered by the council. Even Hanks's old friend Link believed it discordant that a man could be declared innocent of any ethical wrongdoing and yet advised that his conduct has been improper. To Link, "the council itself was guilty of a certain impropriety."[14] There appeared to be reasonable room to doubt the decision.

Hayden himself commented on the committee's methodology. According to Hayden, the actual vote had been seven to seven, but committee members made it unanimous in order to present a unified front. Hayden claimed that even though B. H. Carroll was firmly convinced of Hanks's guilt, he voted for acquittal so that this Dallas matter would finally end. In fact, Hayden insisted that Carroll felt guilty for "whitewashing" Hanks.[15]

There are no records at First Baptist verifying Hayden's allegations, but again according to Hayden, several statements from the ministers who served on the committee make it clear that they did not believe Hanks was innocent of all wrongdoing. Reverend J. R. Clark, for instance, declared, "I do not regard the decision of the council as a vindication of Elder R. T. Hanks. The second specification under the general charge was regarded by the council as fully substantiated. Brother Hanks himself did not regard the decision as a vindication of him, but was very much hurt when it was read to him, exclaiming, 'You have crucified me!'"[16]

Fellow committee member Dr. William Howard reiterated virtually the same statement. He commented that the "decision clearly states that the proof substantiates every material allegation in the second specification, the gravest of all, and yet Brother Hanks vindicated! God in his infinite mercy, save all his servants from such a vindication."[17] Obviously not all the members of the committee were in agreement.

Despite the church-wide agreement to abide by the findings of the committee, not all members in the church kept their word and signed the official referendum exonerating Hanks. Hayden and his co-agitator, co-editor and nephew of R. C. Buckner,[18] A. J. Holt, not only refused to sign, but also kept the First Baptist congregation in turmoil for almost a year over the outcome of the trial.[19] "The friends of Dr. Hanks hurried to cover up the shame of his conduct, but the people will not be fooled," wrote Hayden in a scathing editorial on October 10, 1889. "They know that something happened that unbecomes the character and position of a Minister of the Gospel. They understand that the *Texas Baptist and Herald* desires to publish the truth and will not let things of this sort go unheeded. It is time to face the facts, and let them speak for themselves."

Hanks put up a strong front, declaring he had been cleared by "every tribunal to which he could scripturally appeal."[20] Yet, the pastor, whose wife was deeply disturbed by the ongoing conflict, found no relief. The rumors, despite parishioners' promises to relent, would not die. Finally, the church decided it must take some type of action. The committee's attempt to have it both ways, to absolve Hanks while at the same time rebuking him, only created more problems for the embattled congregation.

For the next several months Hayden and Holt continued to gossip against Hanks in the First Baptist Church. In addition, Hayden gave the church less than full coverage within the pages of the *Texas Baptist and Herald*. Church historian Leon McBeth noted that twenty-four people left the church over the dispute and formed a new congregation in East Dallas. Editors Hayden and Holt gave advice to this church, but did not themselves leave the First Baptist Church. The situation was acute.

Even though many of their fellow congregants left to form a church in East Dallas, and the majority who remained were loyal to Pastor Hanks, Hayden and Holt remained at First Baptist and continued to lambaste their pastor. Finally, on April 3, 1889, the church Disciplinary Committee decided it was time to step in and resolve the matter "involving certain members and the pastor."

Interestingly, Hanks not only brought the charges, but also served on the committee whose job it was to render a verdict. The situation of the defendant serving on the committee that would render the fate of his opposition must have reminded the parishioners of the "Buckner First Church's" victory over the "Link Church." The committee spent two weeks examining the evidence, and on April 17, 1889, at least four official charges were filed against Hayden and Holt. The first accusation concerned the church-wide referendum, signed by the entire church that met to conclude the Hanks scandal. The committee charged that Hayden and Hanks had "signed a written agreement to abide by the decision of the council, which investigated charges against our pastor last September, and they ignored this agreement." Since their names appeared on the referendum, this charge was undeniable.

The second charge, that of lying, was levied more specifically at Hayden than Holt, and the citation was very specific. The charge declared that Hayden had "collected things where they were not according to the written contracts."[21] This charge, even though confusing, concerns Hayden's method of publishing the weekly events of the First Baptist Church within his periodical. He was charged with editorial liberties concerning several of the events published therein. Although many members of the congregation may have felt that this accusation was accurate, the charge cannot be substantiated as far as may be ascertained, and therefore must be considered as little more than a matter of personal opinion.

In a similar manner, the third charge also concerned lying, but in this case it was Hayden's apparent fabrications concerning the original charges against Hanks. The committee reported that Hayden "has said that he had letters from Reverend B. H. Carroll and A. T. Spalding stating that our own Pastor, Reverend R. T. Hanks, was not vindicated by the council who investigated the charges against him, when in fact he had no such letters."[22] Interestingly, Hayden's *Complete Conspiracy Trial Book,* written some years later, cites four letters from members of the committee who had reservations concerning the verdict. Carroll was mentioned in the same context, but no specific letter was included; Spalding was not mentioned at all.[23] If these letters cited in Hayden's text were not fabrications, why not cite the letters of these men? There are at least two possible answers. Hayden may have either lost the letters, or he may have fabricated them. Hayden did not produce the letters, and the committee believed he fabricated their existence.

The fourth charge concerned Hayden's apparent inability to tell the truth. The April 17 *Minutes* state: "Since the proceedings began he has publicly stated that he was anxious to do anything, or to endure any sacrifice for peace." Evidently, several members of the church, in particular Deacons Williams and Marshall, were more than willing to step forward to refute this claim. A trial date was set for the first Wednesday in June. At this point, Hayden and Holt sent letters to B. H. Carroll asking him to attend the trial and speak on their behalf.[24] The defendants appeared to have believed that with the powerful Carroll in their corner, they might have a chance. Carroll failed to respond to their pleas.

At the same time, Hayden and Holt stepped away from the First Baptist Church and joined the recently constituted East Dallas Baptist congregation. Under normal circumstances the dismissal and acceptance of a member into a church would be a very common occurrence. This transfer, however, was not a simple procedure. Hayden and Holt had joined the East Baptist Church without receiving an official letter of dismissal from the First Baptist Church, which at that time was the standard practice among Texas Baptist churches. With the trial looming in the next few weeks, the congregation seemed to be split on what official action it should take concerning the transfer of the defendants' membership. Some members wanted Hayden and Holt separated from the church as quickly as possible. They believed that enough damage had occurred and they wanted the matter to end. Other members realized that a proper letter of dismissal had not been granted and that the ecclesiastical trial should occur before any transfer of membership could take place.

Hayden and Holt had not observed proper procedures for a transferal of membership. Evidently, the First Baptist Church disciplinary committee determined to proceed with the trial regardless of the fact that the two had already joined another church. An article in the May 20, 1889, edition of the *Texas Baptist and Herald* reported that Hayden and Holt had been received into the membership of the East Dallas Baptist Church. Thus, the First Baptist disciplinary committee was forced to decide whether to proceed with the inquiry without the certainty of either their right to proceed or of the defendants' plans to attend the trial.[25]

Several members of the First Church wanted to try the co-editors in absentia. Deacon Williams realized Hayden and Holt had moved beyond the jurisdiction of the First Church. For this reason, "Deacon Marshall moved that the prosecution be contravened and the case dismissed for want of jurisdiction, which was carried."[26] After debating the affair in committees for several months and after many deleterious letters from both churches castigating the position of the other, all of which were published in the *Texas Baptist and Herald* and must have reminded the readership of the old Link-Buckner feud,[27] the First Church bid farewell to the two perceived troublemakers. On June 5, 1889, the names of Hayden and Holt were struck from the membership records of the First Baptist Church of Dallas.

Not surprisingly, Hayden later claimed that his transfer from the First Baptist Church was not an attempt to avoid the trial. *Complete Conspiracy* quotes a letter from Holt in an attempt to prove this point. Even though Hayden and Holt were to be tried together for the same accusations at the First Church, by the mid-1890s Holt had tired of Hayden's actions and joined the faction opposing Hayden. Holt claimed that a meeting composed of ministers from the two churches in question was held in the office of the *Texas Baptist and Herald.* Due to the continued aggrieved state of affairs at the First Church, and "after a laborious and lengthy conference," the two men were allowed to join the East Baptist Church without the usual letters of transfer. Hence, Holt claims they left the First Baptist Church not over the fear of the impending trial and possible negative judgement, but rather for the sake of reconciliation and the reputation of the church. They wanted to spare the church any further embarrassment.[28] In the June 12, 1889, edition of his periodical, Hayden stated that better times were ahead for the First Church because of his decision not to defend his innocence before the bar of the church. After all, according to Hayden, the charges were concocted by Hanks and his cohorts in an attempt to shift attention from the pastor's own guilt.[29] The departure of Hayden and Holt from the First Church was also believed to be the right move by some twenty Texas Baptist ministers who sent Hayden a letter praising him for his actions and pledging their undying loyalty to his cause.[30] Slowly but surely both the

Haydenite faction and the denominational tensions were beginning to gain strength.

Hanks, however, knew the controversy was not over. Realizing that any subsequent ministry of his at the First Baptist Church had been hampered by the negative publicity, he tendered his resignation on June 16, 1889, but it was promptly rejected. Even after several impassioned speeches in which he explained why it was best for the church that he leave, the process of resignation and rejection occurred four times in the ensuing months before the church reluctantly acquiesced.[31]

Despite Hanks's resignation, many First Baptist members transferred their letters of membership to the East Dallas Baptist Church. By August 14 fifty people supporting Hayden's opposition had moved their membership and contributed an open letter to the *Texas Baptist and Herald* delineating their rationale for leaving. The letter, which was caustic and straightforward, stated: "We have long believed that the pastor of the First Baptist Church to be unworthy of his position. The facts developed before the council in December last, the decision of that council, together with evidence more recent, all in our judgement, prove his unworthiness." Despite his most adamant pleas, Hanks could not escape the perception of infidelity.

As evidenced by the preceding quotation, one of the more adroit ways Hayden dealt with his rivals within the pages of *The Texas Baptist and Herald* was through the open letter section of his periodical. Here were published letters, sometimes several at a time, from lay leaders or ministers who backed his various positions. Therefore, when asked if he perpetuated problems by means of his paper, he could merely answer that he was publishing nothing more than the letters of his concerned readership. An excellent example of this methodology may be found in the January 29, 1890, edition of the *Texas Baptist and Herald.* Here the pastor of the Second Baptist Church of Dallas, William Howard, discussed Hayden's abrupt change in church membership and apparent retreat from his forthcoming trial. Howard claimed, "[H]is silence which may seem to some to prove his inability to answer what has been said derogatory to his character, is to those who know the facts in the case the clearest proof of his integrity." From this time forward letters supporting Hayden, and especially those castigating Hanks, found a place of prominence in his newspaper. Of this issue Cranfill stated, "The fight never relented. As long as Hayden had a paper, he reveled in his assaults upon Hanks."[32] Even though Hayden had been a primary figure in the chain of events which had both colored the reputation of Hanks and contributed to his resignation as pastor, Hayden had neither silenced nor banished Hanks. The disheartened pastor remained in Dallas and emerged again in the next phase of the growing controversy.

CHAPTER 4

B. H. Carroll Takes the Lead

THE EMERGING TUMULT AMONG Texas Baptists was paralleled in the early 1890s by economic tumult within the state and nation. The Sherman Silver Purchase Act of 1890 was a major cause of a severe economic downturn that culminated in the "Panic of 1893." With the addition of western states with large silver mining interests, the federal government agreed to purchase 4.5 million ounces of silver each month at market rates. The treasury would then issue notes that were redeemable in either gold or silver. Because so much silver flooded the market, the price of silver went down. Naturally, people wanted to redeem their notes in gold. Soon, the mandatory level of gold to be maintained at the Federal Reserves was met, and gold could no longer be successfully redeemed. With the market in chaos, the Philadelphia, Reading, Northern Pacific, Union Pacific, Atchison, Topeka, and Santa Fe railroads all went bankrupt. The National Cordage Company, the most actively traded stock, went into receivership, 15,000 companies failed, and 500 banks were forced to close their doors. In Texas, the Panic of 1893 hit the city of Dallas especially hard. Five banks closed, cotton prices dropped, and the lumber industry all but vanished.[1]

Dueling Newspapers

Texas and its Baptists were unable to escape from these tough economic times. One of the great fears echoed by Texas Baptists following consolidation was a recurrence of fragmentation. During this period, Hayden, like other leaders of his day, had the unique opportunity to bring the BGCT together in its infancy and secure its unity and its financial stability for following generations. Hayden, however, allowed acrimonious rhetoric and personal desire to dominate his columns, which served instead to damage his journalistic integrity and the undergirding desire for unity.[2] J. B. Cranfill reported that "his assaults upon Hanks and his evident purpose to rule the denomination or subjugate every man who in any wise opposed his policies, led thoughtful leaders to distrust him."[3] Contemporary historian B. F. Riley commented that Hayden, by broadcasting the personal affairs of the First Baptist Church of Dallas to the entire state, demonstrated to everyone his inability to report the news in an unbiased manner.[4] The same could be said of Hayden's treatment of the BGCT and the city of Waco. News favorable to the convention and the central Texas city received scant attention in Hayden's newspaper. Thus, despite the fear that a rival newspaper could rekindle Baptist fragmentation, the leaders of the BGCT realized that perhaps there was a need for a second state Baptist paper. Therefore, "the editorial policies of the *Texas Baptist and Herald*"[5] led to the eventual birth of the *Baptist Standard*.

Even though Hayden had acquired the unified paper, it was never officially endorsed by the BGCT. Hence, no denominational resolution precluded another's inauguration. Therefore, while potentially problematic, there was no official resolution which stated that another paper could not also be supported. Additionally, unity was still valued, and Waco still did not have a paper to advance its policies. Link reported that since Hayden's "paper had proved to be very unsatisfactory to a great many brethren . . . the desires for another paper became deep and widespread."[6] Perhaps Wacoans had been spoiled by the extensive coverage accorded the city in the previous decades by Buckner. This was no longer occurring at such regular intervals.

After these initial salvos had been fired in the Hayden-Hanks scandal, J. H. Boyet and Lewis Holland created *The Baptist News* in

Honey Grove, Texas. In 1889 Holland bought out Boyet's interest in the paper and moved it to Dallas in 1890. Thus, Holland and Boyet had moved their rival periodical right into the heart of Hayden's editorial enterprise. To make the matters more complex, when *The Baptist News* was moved to Dallas, Hanks bought a half interest in the paper from Holland.[7] Hanks and Holland then changed the name of the periodical to *The Western Baptist.* Hanks could now report his side of the story. When discussing his new editorial enterprise, Hanks suggested that he was not merely trying to vindicate himself, but also wanted to advance the united cause of all Texas Baptists. He said, "After a victory had been won, by the tried pastor, before every tribunal to which he could Scripturally appeal, he conceived the notion that Texas Baptists would not have peace until the newspaper autocracy should be broken, and so he resigned the pastorate of the First Baptist Church, Dallas, and announced his purpose of making a broad, religious denominational paper possible." Interestingly, these were not the stated reasons for his resignation as noted in the June 16, 1889, *Minutes* of the First Baptist Church of Dallas. Rather, in his resignation speech he cited his failing health, the emotional pain caused to his wife, and the compromising of his personal ministry, and the church's, by the continued fighting. *The Western Baptist* found immediate acceptance in Dallas. L. R. Elliott suggested that the paper grew "not only because it was ably edited, but because it showed itself friendly toward all the denominational work."[8]

Realizing that he was no longer going to be the proprietor of the sole organ for Texas Baptists, Hayden admonished his readership on April 17 about the inadvisability of forming a new paper: "Now, I warn all brethren throughout the state, at the peril of their good name, not to try in any form or fashion to disturb our united efforts to keep the peace of our Zion. After this union of all our forces in the great state of Texas, it would be fearfully hazardous for any man to try to break this unity by starting another paper or other agencies to carry this work of the General Convention."[9]

Another newspaper would certainly increase the statewide tensions, but at the same time Hayden had no official resolution to stop the birth of the new periodical. As noted in the 1886 regular session of the BGCT, the Convention did not own either of the periodicals and had not endorsed Hayden's unified paper. Still, many Baptists believed that another paper would be more detrimental than helpful.[10] Hayden and Hanks then braced for the newspaper war. Both editors held their peace for two years, largely reporting Baptist news that was helpful to the denomination. Other disputes such as the Martin, Fortune, and Whitsitt controversies drew the attention of Texas Baptists. B. H. Carroll showed a particular interest in each of these controversies and played a significant role in their demise.

Martinism was one of most troublesome doctrinal issues in the last decade of the nineteenth century. The doctrine was named after Matthew Thomas Martin, a young minister who was a member of and who had been licensed to preach by the First Baptist Church of Waco. In 1889 he began to trouble many of his Baptist brethren by pressing the importance of assurance after salvation. McBeth defined Martin's doctrine as the belief "that God gives the Christian such positive assurance of salvation that any doubt at all indicates that a person is not saved."[11] By the early 1880s, Martinism was gaining steam, dozens of Baptists were being re-baptized, and the Texas Baptist leadership was becoming concerned. As his pastor, B. H. Carroll volunteered his efforts to end this heresy. A church council was called at the First Baptist Church of Waco in July 1889 where Martin was asked to renounce his teachings.[12] He refused and his license to preach was rescinded. He relocated to Georgia where another church licensed him to preach.

Martin returned to Texas in 1890 and joined the Marlin Baptist Church, which was a member of the Waco Baptist Association. Located less than thirty miles from Waco, the Marlin Church asked First Waco to restore Martin's credentials. Furthermore, the church told First Waco if it did not restore his license to preach, it would just license him again. B. H. Carroll did not take challenges to his authority kindly, especially in his own backyard. Hence First Baptist Waco denied Martin's request for his license. The Marlin Church then re-licensed Martin, whereupon its membership in the Waco Association was rescinded. In 1893 Martin was called to pastor a Baptist Church in Gloster, Mississippi, where his doctrine found a new audience. The following year the Marlin Baptist Church issued a letter of apology and was permitted to return to the

Waco Association. Even though Martin had left Texas, his doctrines, still perceived as dangerous, were somewhat prevalent in central Texas. In an effort to stem the growth of Martinism, the BGCT passed a resolution condemning anyone who espoused such views and refused to let them be seated at the regular session.[13] The Mississippi Baptist Convention passed a similar resolution in 1897.

Fortunism was another doctrinal problem that plagued Texas Baptists in the 1890s. The doctrine originated from George Fortune, a traveling minister who was invited to preach in the fall of 1891 at the First Baptist Church of Paris, Texas, which was without a pastor. After hearing him preach for several weeks, the congregation called Fortune as the permanent pastor. At that time, Fortune began to espouse heretical teachings from the pulpit. Fortune taught that Christ's death on the cross was not effectual for salvation, there was no personal Satan, original sin did not exist, there was no eternal punishment, and that the Scriptures were not fully inspired by God. Despite these views, Fortune managed to win over the majority of the church to his opinion. The First Baptist Church of Paris then broke all ties with the denomination, refused to use Baptist literature, and permitted non-Baptists to take communion.[14]

A substantial minority of the church's membership was shocked by these teachings and began an investigation into Fortune's past. They found that he had been a Methodist preacher in Illinois, a temperance lecturer in Kansas, and a Baptist preacher in Illinois. It was also widely believed that Fortune's first wife was still alive. With these findings in hand, the minority asked the Lamar Association and several prominent Baptist leaders, such as Rufus Burleson and B. H. Carroll, to hold an ecclesiastical trial to determine who should have the rights to the church building. On February 11, 1896, the Association found Fortune guilty of heresy. Speaking for the council, B. H. Carroll stated that Fortune's doctrines were "a candid, outright, downright, audacious attack on the central, vital doctrines of not only the Baptist faith, but the faith of evangelical Christendom."[15]

The First Baptist Church of Paris ignored the council's ruling and Carroll's condemnation, and Fortune remained pastor until 1897, when he relocated to the Oklahoma Territory to begin a law practice.

Fortune's teachings led to outbursts of heresy in north Texas for several years. In an attempt to stem its growth, a resolution was passed by the BGCT in 1895 condemning Fortunism. The convention also refused to seat anyone at the regular session who held such doctrines.[16]

The Whitsitt Controversy affected the entire Southern Baptist Convention, but Texas Baptists, and in particular B. H. Carroll, helped determine the outcome. William Heth Whitsitt was professor of church history and president of The Southern Baptist Theological Seminary in Louisville, Kentucky. A careful church historian, Whitsitt published several articles promoting the theory that Baptists descended from English Puritanism. While accepted by most reputable scholars in the twenty-first century, this was not the accepted view of many Baptists in the nineteenth century. A central tenet of J. R. Graves's ever-popular Landmark ecclesiology was the belief that Baptists and Baptist churches had existed from the period of John the Baptist. Whitsitt discerned that Baptist teachings date from the New Testament, but the Baptist church itself did not exist until 1608 or 1609.[17]

Whitsitt's teaching led to dissension throughout the Southern Baptist Convention. Baptists wondered how the president of Southern Seminary could promote such a belief. B. H. Carroll remained quiet until 1897, when Southern's trustees refused to take any action against Whitsitt. Carroll, who himself was a trustee at Southern, began to rail against Whitsitt and his anti-Landmark teachings in the *Baptist Standard*.[18] Before long the Texas Baptist champion of orthodoxy had the majority of the state behind him. Carroll managed to get a resolution passed at the 1897 BGCT stating that Whitsitt "ought at once to retire from his position as president, and unless he shall voluntarily retire, the Board of Trustees ought to retire him."[19] When his grassroots movement failed to budge Southern's trustees, Carroll, at the 1898 Southern Baptist Convention, threatened to propose a resolution the following year that would remove the seminary from the Convention. After realizing that Carroll had the votes to get the resolution passed, Whitsitt resigned in the summer of 1898.

By attacking these doctrines and theories that most Texas Baptists found objectionable, B. H. Carroll became the Texas Baptist champion of orthodoxy and the denomination's leading pugilist. He was now a man of considerable stature not only in Texas but throughout the Southern Baptist Convention. Carroll was ready to divert all his attention to the ever-brewing Hayden Controversy.

Remembering the schismatic effects of the Link-Buckner conflict and the role the newspapers played in it, neither Hayden nor Hanks wanted to be the protagonist of a similar split in the denomination. Neither editor wanted to damage his reputation in the pivotal city of Dallas that was finally somewhat at rest after these preceding events. For these reasons, a full-blown newspaper feud between Hayden and Hanks did not occur at this time.

In early March 1892 Holland and Hanks sold *The Western Baptist* to M. V. Smith and J. B. Cranfill, who had served as the Corresponding Secretary of the BGCT from 1888–1892 and was a member of the First Baptist Church of Dallas. The new editors made their intentions clear in the March 3 edition: "In policy the paper will stand by every interest fostered by our people: The Baptist General Convention, our schools, our orphan's home, and every branch of our mission work. Above all, we will stand by the truth as held by our people." Texas Baptist historian L. R. Elliott commented, "The *Baptist Standard* under his [Hanks'] editorial and business management reached lofty heights and provoked widespread comment and commendation throughout the realm of religious journalism."[20] At this point *The Western Baptist,* which had a circulation of about 3,000 subscribers, was renamed the *Baptist Standard* and immediately relocated to Waco. The move to Waco did not surprise Link, who acknowledged that that had been the "original purpose."[21] The city now possessed a newspaper, the denominational offices, Baylor University, and the pulpit ministry of B. H. Carroll. Immediately upon the move, 2,500 new subscribers were added to the subscription list. The *Baptist Standard* was poised to become a powerful newspaper.

Although Hayden appeared to have no serious problems with the new editors, he nonetheless editorialized on occasion that Cranfill's salary was extravagant, his reports incomplete, and that he might be wasting funds that would be better applied to the mission field. To this last matter Hayden gave considerable prominence in his own periodical. Any item that he believed would advance the welfare of state missions he located on either the first or second page of the *Texas Baptist and Herald,* giving it primary attention. In fact, in March 1891 Hayden had provided Corresponding Secretary Cranfill with the *Texas Baptist and Herald's* subscription list so that he might start a missionary letter and solicit funds from the readership.[22] In the following years this specific act would prove to be a source of contention between the two editors, as Hayden would later accuse Cranfill of using this list to obtain subscribers for the *Baptist Standard.*

Hayden also routinely published the complete minutes, proceedings, and financial reports from any entity related to the BGCT. He sincerely believed that every Baptist deserved to know what was occurring within the denomination. This corresponded with the original promise Hayden made to his readership on July 15, 1886, after acquiring the unified paper, "We shall have no denominational secrets, know no favorites, rather each brother and sister in Christ shall be our favorite." At this point in 1893 Hayden still believed Cranfill was a significant improvement over Hanks. Hayden commented, "This we believe to be the next best thing practicable for the Baptists of Texas and another step in the providence of God towards the amelioration of the conditions of our people."[23] Hayden's opinions of these events, however, were soon to change.

Hayden believed that B. H. Carroll's "sore need for a paper in Waco" had now been remedied. In Hayden's opinion, Waco was now complete. Yet, within a year of the periodical's arrival at Waco, M. V. Smith died. Though untrained in the editorial trade, Smith had been deeply respected by Texas Baptists, and the *Baptist Standard* sorely missed his presence. Into the vacancy stepped B. H. Carroll, who in the fall of 1893 had given Cranfill permission to publish his Sunday morning sermons in the *Baptist Standard.* Unlike Hayden, who was primarily popular in north Texas, particularly East Dallas, Carroll was a Baptist giant who commanded attention throughout the bounds of the Southern Baptist Convention. Carroll's sermons and articles lent immediate credibility to the *Baptist Standard.*

In addition, James Bruton Gambrell, a popular editor from Mississippi and future four-time president of the Southern Baptist Convention, frequently contributed articles to the *Baptist Standard.*

This Gambrell did despite Hayden's warnings not to get involved with the *Baptist Standard.* In a circular tract entitled *The Evolution of the Texas Situation,* Gambrell recalled a conversation in which Hayden cautioned, "'If you get into the paper, you'll get hurt.' And then he urged that I have nothing to do with it because I would give strength to the paper and would 'make it more difficult to destroy it.' I have never forgotten the keen, strong impression that bold statement made upon my mind."[24] J. M. Dawson believed Cranfill's acquisition of such prominent Baptist leaders was a financial coup for the *Baptist Standard.*[25] With men such as these as advocates, the *Baptist Standard* was destined to become a powerful newspaper.

In September 1893 Carroll's sermons became a source of conflict between the two papers. Hayden claimed that he received a letter from Carroll's stenographer, a certain Mr. Stewart, offering to sell him the influential pastor's evening sermons at the price of five dollars per transcript. Hayden then contacted Carroll, who agreed that he could purchase the rights to the evening sermons, but the morning sermons were contractually committed to the *Baptist Standard.* Ironically, Hayden suggested that he had no real interest in obtaining Carroll's morning sermons, as he was better heard than read. In addition, he was already publishing the sermons of the Baptist denomination's greatest preacher, Charles Haddon Spurgeon of London, England. Hayden, however, claimed to have acquiesced in favor of the influential Texan in order not to hurt his feelings.[26] A contract was then signed for the evening sermons, and the popularity resulting from the publishing of Carroll's sermons was evenly split between the two Baptist periodicals.

In December, after Hayden had begun publishing the evening sermons, he received a letter from Carroll asking the editor to stop running them in his newspaper.[27] Carroll claimed that his own stenographer was misunderstanding a large portion of the sermons, and thus was failing to record their content accurately. Hayden did not believe this, convinced instead that Cranfill had threatened the stenographer over the *Texas Baptist and Herald's* legal right to publish the evening sermons. Hayden defended his cause in print by claiming that he never wanted to publish the sermons to begin with; however, he insisted that a contract had been signed between the parties and that he still retained the right to publish them. Hayden felt betrayed because Carroll, as a member of the Board and the most influential Baptist in Texas, had backed away from his stance on denominational unity and had endorsed a competing organ. Hayden, therefore, decided to continue to print Carroll's evening sermons rather than accede to their "piratical" tactics.[28] Despite his claim that he never really wanted them, Hayden continued to claim his legal rights to the evening sermons as late as April 26, 1894.

Even though Cranfill, as the owner of the *Baptist Standard,* was the signator of the contracts, Carroll, not Cranfill, presented the other side of the story. As attested by Hayden, Carroll's and Cranfill's main defense against the publication of his sermons was based upon the stenographer's inability to represent them accurately. When asked for a particular reference as to this stenographer's ineptitude, Carroll pointed to only one error that was typographical.[29] Alan Lefever, a B. H. Carroll biographer, points out that the stenographer could not capture Carroll's flair, which was more prominent in his evening sermons.[30] Following the lead of Carroll, Cranfill claimed that when the sermons "were actually published in Hayden's paper, they were so immature and so poorly published that B. H. Carroll wrote to Hayden not to publish any more of them."[31]

The dispute over Carroll's sermons caused Hayden now to acknowledge openly that Carroll was an adversary.[32] The powerful Waco pastor and the ambitious Dallas journalist would never again be on cordial terms. The argument over the sermons also brought Cranfill into the controversy as an ally of Carroll. Prior to this event, Cranfill had been on good terms with Hayden. As he had now aligned himself with Carroll, Cranfill found himself in a perpetual editorial battle with Hayden. As such, Cranfill was forced to deal with Hayden for the remainder of his journalistic career. Texas Baptists began to line up on either side of this debate: advocates of the *Texas Baptist and Herald*, or the *Baptist Standard.*

On January 18, 1894, fire completely destroyed the *Baptist Standard's* office and equipment. The affair was disastrous for Cranfill, who claimed that only the subscription list survived. Since the death of

Smith, Cranfill, with the financial assistance of H. J. Chamberlain, had shouldered the burden of the paper. Despite its popularity, it appeared as if the *Baptist Standard* would not survive, a discouraging prospect for those who supported the Waco paper. Cranfill described these trying days in his *Chronicle*: "These were the darkest hours of my life. Charged with the responsibility of a new enterprise, heavily in debt, conducting a business that was losing money every day, away from home, threatened with blindness, physically ill, and bereft of my loving friend and my most intelligent counselor and sympathizer, the day was almost hopelessly dark."[33]

The local printers union also created trouble for Cranfill. When he moved the paper from Dallas, several families that worked at the *Baptist Standard* came with him to Waco and resumed their old jobs. Since these men were not affiliated with the local union, Cranfill claimed to have received several threats from the Waco Printers Union. Cranfill never directly blamed the Printers Union. Later, Hayden suggested that Cranfill burned the building himself for some "sinister" motive.[34]

Fortunately, Cranfill had purchased a comprehensive insurance policy on the *Baptist Standard.* Thus, despite the total loss of *The Baptist Standard* property, the next issue appeared on its regular date. In an editorial entitled "Tried By Fire," Cranfill estimated the losses at about $12,000.

This placed Cranfill's editorial enterprise in dire straits. Rather than asking for money from his influential friends, in the January 25 issue he asked that his readers renew their subscriptions early. Despite this plea, Cranfill determined that the only way he could save his newspaper was to sell half interest to a silent partner. One of the greatest Baptist philanthropists of the nineteenth century, Colonel C. C. Slaughter of Dallas, rescued Cranfill by purchasing half of the *Baptist Standard* in December 1894. Slaughter's $7500 purchase coincided with the exact amount of money needed to eliminate the debt of the *Baptist Standard.* In return for his joint-ownership, however, Slaughter insisted that the newspaper eventually move to Dallas.[35] This occurred in 1898.

Another influential Baptist who came to Cranfill's aid was J. M. Carroll, the brother of B. H. Carroll. He bought a five-dollar subscription in the magazine, and his name appeared in the periodical as a new subscriber. An adequate but occasionally biased historian, J. M. Carroll claimed that his five-dollar subscription brought him directly into Hayden's line of fire.[36] Four months later, Hayden accused J. M. Carroll of showing favoritism to the *Baptist Standard*, contending that a Board member, such as Carroll, should not show favoritism to either newspaper.[37] Carroll promptly replied, stating: "You charged me with almost wilful criminality because I gave Cranfill five dollars to extend my subscription to *The Standard* soon after it burned, a kindness I would have done for you under similar circumstances."[38] More than likely there were other reasons that also brought about their personal feud. The burning of the *Baptist Standard* would probably have been perceived as just a tragic incident if not for the fact that Cranfill had earlier had so much difficulty keeping financial records straight while serving as the Corresponding Secretary of the BGCT.

There can be no doubt that Hayden and Cranfill were rivals at several levels. Although one paper was published in Dallas and the other in Waco, they competed for the same readership. The disturbance over the sermons and J. M. Carroll's advocacy of the *Baptist Standard* in 1894 proved only to aggravate the situation. It should also be noted that from 1889 until 1892 Cranfill was the Corresponding Secretary of the BGCT. In this role he was responsible for all the financial records of statewide missionary endeavors,[39] and the early 1890s had been lean years as far as statewide budgets were concerned. Cranfill, however, was still very popular. This irked Hayden because it was he, in his newspaper, who had first called attention to Cranfill's alleged financial indiscretions. Yet, Cranfill's *Baptist Standard* was now receiving the support of several BGCT leaders and those loyal to them, while Hayden in the *Texas Baptist Herald* was being snubbed. To rectify this perceived injustice, Hayden decided that further evidence of Cranfill's improprieties must be brought to light.

While Cranfill was filling this new role among Texas Baptists, Hayden continued to print the minutes and financial reports of state-level departments and organizations within the BGCT. He believed that Texas Baptists deserved to know where contributions were spent. In March 1892 Cranfill stepped down as Corresponding Secretary in order to become editor of the *Baptist Standard*.[40] During the

1892 BGCT annual session at Belton, when the official report of the Corresponding Secretary was read, a strange comment appeared: "Let it be remembered that this report includes only the last two quarters of the year, from April 1 to September 30. The reports from the first two quarters were never turned over to the present Corresponding Secretary." In other words, a half a year of financial records was missing. Amazingly, the convention still accepted the report. Even after a called session of inquiry,[41] the Board of Directors did not pry any further into the matter. Texas Baptists trusted Cranfill and the Board believed he had conducted business in a proper manner. And in a *Baptist Standard* editorial of March 3, 1892, Cranfill declared "the mission work was never in better condition." It should be noted that Cranfill was the Corresponding Secretary when he made this claim, and thus may have felt compelled to defend himself against future allegations.

Until Cranfill made this statement, Hayden had made no serious accusation against him. Since the records had been misplaced, Hayden reported that Cranfill should have been more careful. While not yet calling Cranfill an outright embezzler, Hayden was relieved when J. M. Carroll replaced him in 1892. Evidently, Carroll had some accounting skills, and Hayden pointed out in the October 13 publication of the *Texas Baptist and Herald* that he was a significant improvement over the "careless" Cranfill.[42] Hayden suggested that in order to protect the work of the BGCT and make sure such carelessness would not occur again, the Board system needed reform. The accumulation of these events launched what Hayden called the "Reform Movement."

Even though the Board exonerated Cranfill, the fact remained that he had misplaced six months of financial records and Hayden's accusations were becoming commonplace. Cranfill's account of the matter is anything but airtight. He claimed to have given the records to John T. Battle, the Treasurer of the Convention and member of the First Baptist Church of Waco,[43] who had taken them home to Waco to have them bound.[44] While in Waco, Battle had misplaced them. Cranfill later suggested that the aspersions cast on Cranfill deeply disturbed Battle and Battle had spent years looking for them. Suddenly, four years later, Battle remembered where he had placed them. He reclaimed them and turned them over to B. H. Carroll, who immediately had them audited, and the findings were presented to the 1896 BGCT annual session. The records were accepted as authentic, and much to Hayden's amazement, the BGCT exonerated Cranfill once again.[45] In a letter from J. M. Carroll to Cranfill earlier in February 1896, Carroll told Cranfill that in order to clear his name he must get B. H. Carroll and Battle to verify his records. This is the only way he could avoid a charge of embezzlement.[46] These requests were met down to the last detail.

When the "official" books were presented to the BGCT in 1896, Hayden claimed there were several obvious irregularities. The records were copies of the originals. How could this occur if Battle had handed over the exact copies that he had lost for proper auditing? In addition, the books, rather than written in Cranfill's hand, as he claimed, were penned by four or five different people. Moreover, the new Corresponding Secretary, J. M Carroll, claimed to have given Cranfill $2500 to supplement the salary of some underpaid state missionaries. According to Hayden, this money was neither accounted for nor recovered. Furthermore, at the conspiracy trial in 1902, Cranfill claimed that he had not seen the books after they had been lost in 1892 until recovered by Battle in 1896. Yet, when urged by several Haydenites at the 1894 Marshall Convention to show the books, Cranfill had claimed he had them with him and would present them later that day. The books, according to Hayden, did not appear at the Marshall BGCT.[47]

When coupled with the mysterious burning of the *Baptist Standard* and with what Hayden believed to be an inordinate insurance claim, Cranfill was targeted by Hayden.[48] Despite Hayden's suspicions, Cranfill himself stated that Hayden did not begin attacking him until after 1893.[49] But in the October 25, 1894, issue of the *Texas Baptist and Herald* Hayden was certain that the evidence of embezzlement against Cranfill was overwhelming. The unexplained burning of the *Baptist Standard* only added to his suspicion.

As the editor of the *Baptist Standard*, Cranfill used his periodical to defend himself and his compatriots early in the affair when the situation began to garner attention. At this point the Hayden Controversy took an important turn. Whereas a great deal of the problem had accrued from the statewide events represented at First Baptist Dallas and the location of the unified paper, Hayden now gave his full attention to the apparent problems with the manner in which the Board of the BGCT was handling its finances.

Only after the accumulation of these incidents did Hayden begin to question many of the events at hand separately. One should also note that Hayden did not question the Board System itself, but rather the manner by which the current members, excluding himself, were handling its affairs. While he began to present these matters in the *Texas Baptist and Herald*, Cranfill defended the Board members in the *Baptist Standard*, the latter of which was, by 1894, quickly becoming the unofficial voice of the BGCT.[50] Except for R. C. Burleson, Hayden reported that all of the influential members of the BGCT were flocking to Cranfill's side where their various agendas would find ample coverage within his periodical.[51]

CHAPTER 5

Hayden's Reform Movement

DESPITE HIS BELIEF THAT J. M. Carroll was a far better Corresponding Secretary than J. B. Cranfill, Hayden proclaimed that times were lean and that the salaries of the Board were excessive. He constantly belittled the increased salary of J. M. Carroll. Hayden suggested that Carroll's $400 salary increase over his predecessor had been secured by his brother and that nepotism was at the heart of the matter. As early as the March 1, 1894, edition of his *Texas Baptist and Herald*, Hayden was already taking Carroll's salary to task. "At a time when many are in dire want, and the missionaries are suffering untold hardships," Hayden argued "Dr. Carroll had been drawing a large salary." Two weeks later Cranfill defended Carroll in his periodical. After describing Carroll's enormous statewide responsibilities, Cranfill asserted: "We do not believe that any man, environed as he has been, could have done a greater work for the cause of missions than he has been blessed of God to do."

Though several offices had been combined into the Corresponding Secretary's duties in 1893, Carroll had received a $400 dollar raise over his predecessor. One should note, however, that he was doing the work previously done by four men.[1] Hayden believed that during these trying financial times everyone should be accepting as salary only what was needed. After all, before being consolidated into the position of Corresponding Secretary, the Secretaries of Home Missions, Foreign Missions, State Missions, and Minister's Relief Work only made $1600 dollars a year.

During the 1893 regular session of the BGCT in Gainesville, several matters were discussed in an all-night session. Before the Board convened that night, Carroll, perhaps realizing that Hayden would attack him on this issue, stated, "Brethren, I understand that there are some brethren who think my salary is too large. I now relieve you of any obligation as to amount. Make it whatever is just and right. And now I agree to accept it."[2] The Board, of which Hayden was a member, then unanimously voted that J. M. Carroll's salary would remain at $2500.

Even though Hayden evidently voted in favor of the increased salary, he did not lessen his attack against the Board. Combining the controversy over B. H. Carroll's sermons, Cranfill's secretarial carelessness, J. M. Carroll's "inordinate salary," and a general growing dissatisfaction with what was perceived to be "Waco dominance" of Texas Baptist leadership, Hayden developed a plan of financial reform for the Board of the BGCT. On April 2, 1894, he sent a letter to each member of the Board announcing his plans to make several motions at the Board meeting on April 9. The alleged objective was to end the Board's wanton wastefulness. Hayden believed, because "our missionaries are suffering almost to starvation and the expenses of the Board are in excess of any expenses ever before incurred by the Board. This, as it seems to me, should be remedied by some means, fair and satisfactory to all concerned, so as if possible to bring the expenses of the Board for salaries, clerk hire, etc., back to the old figure."[3] Shortly after mailing this letter, Hayden published his plan of reform in the April 6 edition of his newspaper. His backers responded favorably, but there was also opposition, and soon Texas Baptists would again polarize.

The Board immediately reacted and held a closed called session on April 9, 1894, in Waco. Before the meeting convened, B. H. Carroll wanted to know who had expressed a desire to keep the proceedings closed. After demanding an answer from Hayden, the editor stated that it had been J. M. Carroll who had made the request. Hayden stated that J. M. Carroll had requested a closed-door session because he did not want anyone to know his salary "out of a fear it would damage the missionary work."[4] B. H. Carroll was incensed over this statement, and the meeting was delayed several hours so that the Carroll brothers could compose themselves.

After the meeting convened, B. H. Carroll rose and stated that if anyone had an objection to the manner in which the Board was conducting its business, it should be written down and distributed to the members. Hayden immediately complied and reiterated his original complaints, registered in his April 2 circular letter. He asked the committee to answer five specific complaints that had been leveled against the Board:

> 1. Whether or not the debt of this board has increased or diminished during the last year.
> 2. Whether or not the expenses of this board are in excess of any ever before incurred by it.
> 3. Whether or not the missionaries have increased or decreased or diminished during the past year.
> 4. Whether or not any information necessary to secure the hearty co-operation of the brethren, relating to our work as a board, has been withheld from the brethren and the churches.
> 5. If the committee finds that the debt of the board has increased, its expenses greater than ever before incurred, and the number of missionaries has diminished, then the reasons, if any, therefore, and whether or not the present scale of expenses are necessary to the efficiency of our work and it maintenance at its present standard of excellence.[5]

A committee was then appointed to determine the legitimacy of these claims. After several hours of careful deliberation, the committee reached its verdict, disagreeing with Hayden on every count. The committee's results showed that the expenses of the Board were reasonable; that there were more missionaries than before; that they were not starving; and the Board's debt had actually decreased. His charges refuted by the facts, Hayden himself moved the adoption of the findings.

B. H. Carroll knew that times were difficult on the field, even if the missionaries were not actually starving. The Panic of 1893 had severely damaged the BGCT's budget. He also wanted to remove any possible blame for their hardships from the Board, if possible. Hence, he offered a resolution stating that their troubles were not due to the Board as much as "drought, and other local conditions in their several fields, rendering the local brethren and churches unable to make their usual contributions for their support." The resolution was adopted by the Board. According to Hayden, the committee asked him not to mention the dispute again in his newspaper until the next regular session of the BGCT at Marshall in October 1894.[6]

This agreement was soon broken, but neither Hanks, B. H., nor J. M. Carroll fired the first volley. A new entity now entered the editorial fray. The April 13, 1894, edition of the *Fort Worth Gazette* published an article entitled, "They Sat on Dr. Hayden."[7] The man responsible was Cranfill. The article had been published on Cranfill's press in the office of the *Baptist Standard,* and it disclosed all the acrimonious details the members of the Board had agreed not to have published. By publishing this article, Cranfill may have hoped that B. H. Carroll would be offended and the most powerful Baptist in Texas would be forced to take the lead in the destruction of Hayden.

Hayden later stated that Cranfill not only broke their agreement of silence, but that he also had perverted the account. According to Hayden, the editorial portrayed him as an insanely jealous man who, when denied Carroll's evening sermons, had decided to "make the Carrolls uncomfortable."[8]

After returning to Dallas and reading the *Gazette*, Hayden felt no obligation to remain quiet, for Cranfill had already broken the agreement. Thus, he renewed his tirades against the Board, particularly J. M. Carroll. In the very next edition of his periodical on April 19, Hayden once again asserted that the "missionaries were starving," continuing a theme he presented in subsequent editions. His articles hinted that the

Board was living lavishly while the missionaries were living in squalor. In an especially irate issue on June 14, Hayden stated that J. M. Carroll would forsake every missionary in the state for a few hundred dollars.

It would seem that Hayden had good cause to be provoked. It was Cranfill, not Hayden, who first disclosed what the Board had done. But Hayden seems to have overreacted. This overreaction led Hayden to suspect there was a conspiracy within the BGCT opposed to him and that the Carrolls and Cranfill were united against him.

Cranfill immediately fired back in the September 6 issue of the *Baptist Standard* by arguing that Hayden's sowing of discord and lies were the sole reason Texas Baptists no longer trusted the Board of Directors. Hayden's October 25 editorial contradicted Cranfill's statement. Hayden claimed that, "I want to say right here that whatever of good has come out of this agitation belongs to the 'reform paper' introduced at the April meeting of the Board." In an apparent attempt to defend his actions, Hayden stated in the August 30 edition that he never made any personal allegations against anyone on the Board, just their salaries. As attested to in his prior statement concerning J. M. Carroll, Hayden was mistaken. Cranfill began to publish even more letters to the editor that favored the position of the Board and J. M. Carroll. In the September 6 issue of the *Texas Baptist and Herald*, Hayden once again laid out in detail his plans for reform that he would present at the Marshall BGCT session in October. By announcing his plans a month in advance, Hayden hoped his reforms would gain an audience and that he would garner additional votes at the Convention.

While this rhetoric mounted in intensity, the Board held a second called session in Waco on June 26–27. Illness prevented Hayden's attendance, but he was represented by Reverend Pinkney Hawkins, who remained virtually silent during the entire session.[9] Neither side attempted to quell the open hostilities that had erupted in the periodicals, but the lines were beginning to harden between the two factions.[10] B. H. Carroll, representing the anti-Hayden faction, castigated members of the Board who owned newspapers that were not organically connected to the BGCT and who were disrupting the work of the Convention. He demanded a cessation of all hurtful accusations against the Board, reasoning that just because a person was a Board member and an editor was no justification for using his influence to destroy the mission work.[11] Though these comments were clearly directed at Hayden and his growing movement, both Hayden and Cranfill were printing every acrimonious detail about the other faction in each edition. If one newspaper fired an article against the other, the opposing publication answered with an immediate and escalated reply. For instance, an editorial in the July 5, 1894, edition of the *Baptist Standard* claimed that the articles published by S. J. Anderson, a strong Haydenite, and S. A. Hayden "had seriously crippled the mission work." In the September 13, 1894, Hayden responded by publishing a letter from J. J. F. Lockhart which stated: "Every Bro. that I meet say amen to brother Hayden's reform in salary and clerk hire. It ought to have been broken several years ago. The mission cause would have been a great better off. If brethren who are filling positions cannot accept a reduction in salary let them step down and someone else will take their place under the reform move. God bless the *Texas Baptist and Herald* in its work for reform and justice for all." Obviously, both editors were equally guilty of damaging the mission work in Texas, for such remarks continued well into the October 1894 regular session of the BGCT at Marshall.

Possibly the strangest episode between the two factions took place in September 1894 at a mission rally in Dallas. This event demonstrates the depth of open animosity that now existed between B. H. Carroll and Hayden and how each manipulated the story to garner statewide sympathy. Both Carroll and Hayden were present at the rally; no debate between the men had been scheduled, but Carroll, who was not scheduled to speak, was asked to discuss the statewide mission problem. Following the discussion, Carroll proposed that an offering be taken to supplement the missions effort. On these details Hayden and Carroll both agreed, but their accounts differed sharply thereafter.

Carroll claimed that right before the prayer he heard someone speaking, and when he turned around he saw "the editor of the *Texas Baptist and Herald* standing behind him." He then stated "that golden spirit was gone" and that no prayer was offered at all. Out of the desperate need for mission funds, an offering was still taken. Carroll then stated in the September 13 issue of the *Standard* that Hayden remarked that people should feel free to give because none of the money would go to J. M. Carroll's salary; that even though B. H. Carroll had just slandered him in the sermon, he still wanted the offering to be taken. Carroll stated that this was the end of the affair, and that had he any idea that such would occur he would never have agreed to participate in such a service.

Hayden, on the other hand, suggested that since the meeting was held in Dallas, Carroll had known that the congregants were readers of the *Texas Baptist and Herald.* Hayden insinuated that Carroll might have hoped to extract some revenge on the editor within his own readership. Hayden then claimed that he wanted to reconcile himself with Carroll before the prayer began, since his sermon would have damaged the offering. He then offered him the "right hand of fellowship," which Carroll flatly rejected, stating, "I never mix services." Hayden, however, admitted in the September 20 issue of the *Texas Baptist and Herald* that he did state that people should give freely, since none of it would go to the salary of J. M. Carroll.

More than likely this encounter was neither as planned nor as debilitating to the BGCT efforts as claimed by each of the participants. The problem, however, was that both men had immediate access to a newspaper, which printed opposing views of the same event. It was left to the readers of each to decide who was telling the truth. This event would sporadically appear in each of the newspapers for years afterwards. Neither minister was willing to accept any portion of blame for the incident; instead, each man continually summoned representatives who supported his side of the story.[12] This unfortunate incident was fresh in the minds of the readership of both newspapers, and the regular session of the BGCT at Marshall was now less than a month away. Each group began to prepare for the inevitable conflict.

On October 10, 1894, the regular session of the BGCT at Marshall was called to order. By this time two clear parties had emerged within the BGCT: the Board Party, whose adherents held a deep reverence for the Carroll brothers, Waco, and the *Baptist Standard;* and the Haydenite Party, whose followers distrusted the Board, were tired of the perceived Waco dominance, and backed the *Texas Baptist and Herald.* Since the efforts toward reform had been engaged earlier in

April, each faction had attempted to garner as many messengers as possible for the meeting. If the Haydenites could outnumber the Board supporters, the reforms would have a better chance of adoption and Hayden would be exonerated. If not, Hayden could suffer a setback.

Each side sought the support of the convention. For the prior two years R. C. Burleson, president of Baylor University, had been the President of the BGCT. Though the majority of the more prominent members of the BGCT, such as the Carrolls, Hanks, and Cranfill, had openly aligned themselves against Hayden, Burleson was an open supporter.[13] A defeat of the beloved president of Baylor University, therefore, was vital for Board dominance. After careful consideration, the Board selected R. C. Buckner as its candidate. Despite his unfortunate involvement in the church split at the First Baptist Church of Dallas a decade earlier, the founder of the orphanage was, by this time, perceived statewide as a trusted leader.

The BGCT messengers voted for the president after the candidates made their speeches. The final tally stood Buckner 232, Burleson 92. This was a tremendous setback for Hayden, who had counted on Burleson for the continued support of his reforms. For the remainder of the decade Hayden would depict this vote as a lack of appreciation for one of the great Baptist pathfinders in Texas. Hayden had always supported Burleson, but now he took up Burleson's causes with an almost crusading spirit.

Though popular, Burleson's loss can be attributed to several factors. He had openly aligned himself with Hayden, which hurt him in his own hometown of Waco, given the immense influence of B. H. Carroll. Buckner, on the other hand, had been busy working with the orphanage since 1877. With the Buckner-Link affair at the First Baptist Church of Dallas now behind him, no one, including Hayden, openly questioned the character of "Father" Buckner, or questioned his election as president of the BGCT. A testimony to Buckner's standing and popularity among Texas Baptists was his election as president of the BGCT for the next twenty consecutive years. Though closely associated with the Carroll brothers and Cranfill, he had not been involved in the newspaper quarrels of the recent years. Thus, quite possibly many of the messengers regarded Buckner as a peacemaker between the two camps.[14] The official *Proceedings* of the 1894 BGCT clearly attribute Buckner's election to his perceived non-partisanship.

After electing Buckner president, the Board moved to its regular business. The reports demonstrate that the previous debts had been alleviated and that the financial records were exact. Texas appeared to be shedding its financial troubles, and prospects for the future work were bright. The BGCT estimated its membership to be in the neighborhood of 300,000. J. M. Carroll was again elected Corresponding Secretary. His ailing wife's health soon forced him to resign whereupon Marshall Daniel Early replaced him. However, some trouble could not be avoided. In the midst of these routine and positive proceedings, several of the Haydenites demanded to review the controversial books of 1892 that Cranfill claimed to have lost. While asserting that he had them in his possession, Battle refused to offer them for inspection. Before the end of the month, Hayden had once again reminded his readership on October 25 of these missing records and the suspicious manner in which the *Baptist Standard* had been burned down.

Furthermore, Hayden attempted to move forward with his reform package, which included lowering the Board's salary, opening the financial records to public inspection, and reducing the BGCT's debt. Momentum seemed clearly against the editor, since the Board had been exonerated of wrongdoing and Burleson had been defeated as president. Hayden approached the platform and, after addressing the messengers for either six[15] or fourteen hours,[16] a vote was taken. Hayden's reforms were rejected. The Convention then passed a resolution insisting that those on the Board who were determined to undermine the majority should acquiesce for the good of the Convention. To the messengers at the annual session, it appeared that Hayden's editorial influence and the reform movement had both died on the Marshall Convention floor. For the remainder of the year and well into 1895, Hayden lessened his attacks on the Board. Whether he had personally accepted the convention's mandate is not known, but his paper, like that of Cranfill, seemed to be filled with the heresies of Martinism and Fortunism.[17]

CHAPTER 6

Winner Takes It All

ALTHOUGH TROUNCED AT MARSHALL, Hayden refused to give up. To his call for reform he now added sensational charges: J. B. Cranfill was an embezzler, B. H. Carroll was an autocrat, R. T. Hanks was an adulterer, and J. M. Carroll was preoccupied with the love of money.[1] In addition, President Buckner was under the Board's control. Hayden rarely said anything negative about the Board system itself, but rather continually questioned the honesty of several of its perpetual members. During the next six years Hayden intensified his attack, contending that Board members rather than the churches were making all of the decisions for the BGCT. This argument now became a crusade for "Baptist polity." Although the Hayden Controversy was largely founded on old personal grievances, it increasingly revolved around ecclesiology.

Hayden made his position clear through the columns of his paper. On the one hand, he suggested that those who supported the Board party were in fact supporting an episcopal hierarchy that closely resembled Roman Catholicism. On the other hand, he argued that those who supported his own claims were not against the Board system but rather against an episcopal hierarchy that controlled the BGCT. He advocated a greater understanding for his readership of the affairs at the state level and a louder voice for local churches. With each successive year from 1895 until 1901, Hayden's charges against the Board grew louder and more caustic. The Board always reciprocated in like manner. The result was a bitter denominational feud waged in the columns of the rival newspapers and on the floor of the annual Convention gathering.

For a short time following his rout at the Marshall Convention, Hayden ameliorated somewhat his anti-Board rhetoric. R. C. Burleson, however, was scorned by the loss of his presidency. Probably for this reason, Burleson continued to accuse Cranfill of embezzlement. These public accusations became so pronounced that Cranfill was forced to write a letter to Burleson warning him that if he did not desist in these unproven accusations he would sue him for libel.[2] Hayden, however, remained largely silent. Some Texas Baptists suggested that Hayden had finally realized his defeat.[3] Others, however, believed he was merely biding his time and waiting for new opportunities to attack his enemies.[4]

Cranfill also lessened his attacks on Hayden. One reason for the momentary calm may have been the more pressing debate over the problems of Martinism and Fortunism. These heresies matters grated against traditional Baptist doctrine and demanded immediate attention. So, Hayden and the Board put their differences aside and united against this internal threat. In 1895 rarely did an issue of the *Baptist Standard* and the *Texas Baptist and Herald* reach publication without an attack on those who held these doctrines. With the 1895 regular session of the BGCT at Belton quickly approaching, both Hayden's followers and those of the Board wanted these doctrinal controversies to cease.

The 1895 regular session of the BGCT proved to be monumental. It appeared that all of the messengers, except the Martinites and Fotunenites, were united against these doctrinal issues. The Hayden-Board squabble took second place to this danger. Even before the opening formalities were complete, a resolution was offered and adopted by a deacon named B. Badger, which stated:

> Whereas, Baptists recognize Articles of Faith as expressions of what they believe the [*sic*] Bible teaches on doctrines distinguishing us from people of other faiths, and,
> Whereas, Baptist churches in this country have subscribed to the declaration of principles as set forth in "Pendleton's Manual" and "Hiscox's Directory" and
> Whereas, a school has appeared among us who openly say they do not believe the expressions as taught in said Articles of Faith are supported by the Word of God and do not endorse them, and,
> Whereas, this Convention is supposed to be composed of delegates from churches endorsing and teaching God's word in harmony with said Articles of Faith, therefore be it
> Resolved, that we seat as delegates only those who come from regular missionary Baptist churches subscribing to the Articles of Faith.[5]

Evidently believing the resolution was not sufficiently stringent, Hayden, A. H. Mitchell, and E. R. Carswell presented an amendment that stated:

> Whereas, the body is based on what Baptist Articles on Faith declare, therefore,
> Resolved, that no one be recognized a member of this body who holds and teaches any doctrine contrary to them of such import as that no Christian has ever doubted or ever can doubt he is saved, known as a part of "Martinism"—or that Christ is not the believer's substitute, penalty and righteousness—a doctrine held by "Fortunism."[6]

As it became obvious that official action by the Convention was pending with the intent to eliminate these doctrinal issues, at least one person, A. H. Mitchell, realized the inherent power the Convention would gain over the local churches because of this resolution. If the Convention could pass an amendment that could refuse a messenger a seat beforehand, how long would it be before it could declare itself eligible to unseat a messenger after the convention had begun, and with whom it disagreed? With this in mind, Mitchell offered the following amendment to the prior resolution:

> Whereas, this Convention is composed of delegates messengers from the sovereign Baptist churches, and said sovereignty is lodged in each of the churches, and here represented only by said messengers or delegates, and all meet upon a common level; therefore be it
> Resolved, that it is the judgement of this body that it alone can pass upon the
> denominational fitness of its constituents, that is, when any issue is raised, in the meetings of its annual sessions demanding immediate action.[7]

Mitchell wished to make clear that although the doctrinal matters of Martinism and Fortunism must be undertaken by the Convention, it was still the individual church's responsibility to determine the adequacy of its own messengers. However, since the churches that supported Martinism and Fortunism were not likely to denounce their own messengers, it was the body of sovereign churches, which met as equals, that held responsibility for determining the adequacy of messenger representation. Mitchell's resolution, which failed adoption, demonstrated his belief that the sovereign churches, gathered as equals at the Convention, should make the decision on eligibility and not the Convention itself.

The wording of the official resolution would prove to be very important. The official doctrinal standard for the BGCT came from two sources, Pendleton's *Church Manual*[8] and Hiscox's *Directory*,[9] both of which asserted that no power was to supersede the authority of the local church. A five-man committee was then formed to write a resolution reflecting this stance. After deliberation the committee proposed:

> Resolved, 1, that it is the sense of this Convention that Article II, Section 1, of the Constitution sufficiently expresses the fact that the Convention is composed of persons chosen

> by churches, associations and missionary societies as their messengers, and that when said persons are convened they, and not the churches, are the Convention.[10]

This resolution passed by an overwhelming majority, which included Hayden's vote in the affirmative. The fear of Martinism and Fortunism led to the acceptance of this resolution, since the second and third resolutions forbade the advocates of unpopular movements from being seated as messengers. The three resolutions were voted on as one. Thus, if one wanted to prevent the Martinites and Fortunites from being seated, one must affirm the entire resolution. Perhaps the majority of the BGCT messengers were caught up in the moment of removing the power of representation from the messengers with diverse doctrinal positions, but by passing the entire resolution the local church abrogated much of its influence with the Convention.

Furthermore, if one examines Article II Section 1 of the BGCT constitution, the interpretation of those who penned the resolution fell short of its initial intention. The article states: "This body shall be composed of Messengers from regular Baptist Churches, and Associations of Baptist Churches, and Baptist Missionary Societies cooperating with the Convention."[11] Several irregularities occurred when the Convention messengers accepted the new interpretation. Nowhere in this article does it state that, when seated, the messengers comprised an authoritative body. The key word in the article was "cooperating." By passing this resolution, the Convention had dissolved the authority of the local church while the Convention was in session. The acceptance of this resolution now allowed the Convention to remove anyone, not just those with diverse doctrinal views, from its midst if majority ruled.

Moreover, the article did not coincide with the teachings found in Pendleton's *Church Manual* or Hiscox's *Directory*. In this regard, Pendleton's *Church Manual* states that "the power of a church cannot be transferred or alienated, and that church action is final."[12] Hiscox's *Directory* maintains that "both the *right* and *responsibility* of administering this government Christ has committed to each church. No others can lawfully take these from them, nor can they commit them to any other hands. They cannot transfer the government to officers, not to a part of the members, nor to any body of men external to the church."[13]

Third, men who held Landmark ecclesiology, such as J. B. Cranfill,[14] B. H.[15] and J. M.[16] Carroll and J. B. Gambrell, who later supported the referendum,[17] voted to deny a local church's sovereignty and place it at the discretion of the Convention in this sweeping resolution.

Of the three points, the third is the most puzzling. For the Carroll brothers and Cranfill, whose denominational writings indicate a strong belief in the sovereignty of the church, the question is why they were willing to sacrifice any degree of local church sovereignty. In particular, Cranfill editorialized in the pages of the November 28, 1895, edition of the *Baptist Standard*, that "Associations are mere expediencies, devised by human wisdom, and are not like scriptural churches divine institutions." The ensuing year the *Standard* again stated in its July 30 issue, "The only Christian organizations spoken of in the Bible are the churches of Christ. They are the only religious bodies that have any ecclesiastical authority." As late as July 6, 1897, B. H. Carroll reported to the readers of the *Baptist Standard* that "the church is a divine institution. It is the only visible religious organization that is of specific divine appointment." In Carroll's 1913 work *Baptists and Their Doctrines*, he goes so far as to state that the church is "a pure democracy" and "the supreme court in Christ's Kingdom."[18]

Only two reasons for their abridgement of local church autonomy may be offered. In order to build the Texas denomination according to their vision, they realized that a centralized Board was vital. These men were builders of denominational enterprises and institutions. They appeared to have been willing to adjust their doctrinal stances in order to achieve this goal. Hayden was against men who would set aside their principles for personal political expediency. Moreover, if they were willing to suspend ecclesiology for the sake of control, they would be able to remove Hayden from their midst.

A factor that helped to lessen tensions at the 1895 Belton Convention was the resignation of J. M. Carroll as Corresponding Secretary. He was replaced by his former assistant, M. D. Early, who was reelected at the Belton Convention. Hayden gave approval of him in the January 31, 1895, edition of the *Texas Baptist and Herald,* writing: "The whole denomination should rally to support him. It is believed that he will avoid the entangling alliances which have hitherto embarrassed our work." Hayden viewed the removal of Carroll as a step toward Board reform.

With Martinism and Fortunism put to rest, Hayden returned to his attacks on the Board. On October 24, 1895, not a month after the conclusion of the Belton Convention, Hayden editorially repudiated his Belton vote, although it was, of course, too late to change the outcome. The diatribes in the *Texas Baptist and Herald* picked up in the March 12 issue when Hayden and S. J. Anderson, his co-editor and old cohort from the First Baptist Church of Dallas, joined together to resurrect an old theme: the Board's wasting of money. On the same day that Hayden resumed his printed attacks, B. H. Carroll retorted in the pages of the *Baptist Standard* that if Hayden's adherents did not like the policies of the BGCT they were welcome to leave. A short week later in the March 19 edition of his periodical, Hayden reminded his readers that "the Boards are made up of men who do not possess infallibility." From March until October articles such as these dominated the *Texas Baptist and Herald* until time for the 1896 BGCT in Houston. Except for urging messengers to report at the approaching Houston Convention to defeat Hayden and his tactics, acerbic editorials were not as prominent in the *Baptist Standard,* which was, for the most part, quiet. However, as the October Convention loomed ever closer, Carroll wrote a scathing editorial against Hayden in the October 8 publication of the *Standard,* and the leadership of the Convention became increasingly aware that formative action was necessary to stop Hayden's further chronic disruptions to the body politic. Apparently, Convention leaders decided the Houston Convention was the proper venue for this effort.[19]

Amid heavy tension, the 1896 regular session of the BGCT was called to order on October 9 with an unprecedented 493 messengers registered.[20] Once again Buckner was elected president, and Anderson E. Baten and George Washington Truett (1867–1944) were chosen to serve as the Convention Secretaries. The opening business was conducted as usual with a resolution promoting coeducation at Baylor University, which passed without difficulty. The Convention's attention then turned to G. W. Truett and his secretarial report on missionary endeavors. He noted that there had been serious charges leveled against the Board that had led to a sharp decline in financial support. The discussion then focused on the outlook for the upcoming year. In this report that minced no words, Truett said:

> For several years past an agent has been at work in our state and undermining the mission work, drying up the mission spirit, and sowing down our once fertile fields with salt. That agent has persistently, ruthlessly and openly, in public print attacked the board, its methods and work, charging it directly and indirectly, and various methods of innuendo and insinuation, with misappropriation, wanton extravagance and reckless waste of public funds. Through an unwitting instrument, unconscious of what he was led by him to sign, he has published virtual charges of embezzlement against the secretary, and by fair implication the board itself. With this agent nothing pertaining to this work is sacred or ever settled. He evinces open disrespect of the decisions of this body, going back each year behind its approved and finished work to dig up and galvanize such issues or events as by his unrighteous use of them may best contribute to add to the general distrust, discord and divisions he himself engendered . . . Is there no end of patience? Shall sickly sentimentality about peace forever usurp the throne of justice? Shall we wait until the mission cause, now bleeding, is stamped out of existence? Who, then, is this agent? His name is S. A. Hayden of Dallas.[21]

Following this dramatic statement, Truett, speaking for the majority of the Board, asked the Convention messengers to deny Hayden a seat in the Convention. Six members of the Board filed an official protest, believing that a man could not be tried on the Convention floor. The protest stated: "Believing that it is not competent for the board of directors, under the constitution of the convention, to consider, as a board, many of the things incorporated in the above report, or to arraign any person or persons for trial before this convention, we ask that this, our protest, be inseparably attached to the report, and be printed, in the minutes of the convention."[22] Despite the protest, Hayden had been charged with sowing discord, and a motion was made in an attempt to arraign him before the Convention. The motion, which was eventually denied, created so much unrest that the entire Monday session was dedicated to Hayden's trial.

Each side was given two hours to present its case. Hayden spoke first. After apologizing for stating to a local paper that he was going to bring a policeman along with him for protection, he then claimed that the charges against him were nothing more than an attempt to stifle his reforms. He also brought several witnesses who supported his interpretation of the charges.[23] J. B. Scarborough, a Baylor trustee and Board member, and B. H. Carroll spoke on behalf of those who wished to deny Hayden a seat.[24] Perhaps believing that the best evidence against Hayden was the *Texas Baptist and Herald*, they read to the messengers several of his particularly harsh editorials against the Board.

Following the debate, Walter Tynes, a contributing writer for the *Texas Baptist and Herald,* admitted that several of the acrimonious articles presented as evidence of engendering dissension were not written by Hayden but by himself; thus, it would be unfair to try a man for articles he did not actually write. Even though Hayden was the editor of the newspaper, and he made executive decisions about what was to be printed each day, Tynes's argument appeared to carry some weight. Following Tynes's statement, opposition to the action began to rumble throughout the auditorium. Thirty-three messengers, led by R. C. Burleson, signed a referendum that stated the belief that it was wrong to unseat a fellow messenger who had been duly elected by his church.[25]

Perhaps sensing that a formal split was about to rupture the Convention, O. S. Lattimore proposed that the Convention censure Hayden, warn him against any future unwarranted attacks, but allow him to be seated as a messenger. Cranfill cited the rationale for the call for censure rather than disenfranchisement at this time: "At that point, Hayden's strength in Texas was great. He still presided over the destinies of the old and long established newspaper and had a very strong following, including R. C. Burleson, one of the rarest men of any period of Texas Baptist history. His alignment with Hayden was the strongest asset that Hayden ever had at any time."[26]

While the Hayden trial dominated the 1896 Convention, other events complicated the situation. The lost financial records of Cranfill's last six months as Corresponding Secretary were found and presented to the Convention as complete and accurate.[27] Cranfill had been officially exonerated of any wrongdoing by the 1892 Convention, but Hayden had never been satisfied with his innocence. His attacks upon Cranfill never relented.

In addition, against his wishes, M. D. Early was reelected Corresponding Secretary. Despite being viewed as a competent Corresponding Secretary, Early was tired of the battle and made it clear that as soon as someone competent was found who could take his place he was going to resign. Apparently Hayden's stings had taken a toll on Early.[28] Early's resignation would allow a new and powerful member of the anti-Hayden party to enter the fray.

Another complication was the presence of J. B. Gambrell, who was a guest at the Convention.[29] He was partisan to the Convention model that the Board of the BGCT was attempting to build. In fact, he had helped bring into existence the Southern Baptist Convention's Sunday School Board in 1891. He had also developed some reputation as an ecclesiological warrior and was well known among Texas Baptists.

After the Convention was over, Hayden completely ignored the censure and resumed his attacks until the ensuing Convention. Not a month passed but that Hayden declared in the October 29 issue of his newspaper that the American principle of free speech was being trampled upon. "Shall free speech be denied a Baptist concerning the management of Baptist affairs?" Hayden asked. A week later Hayden once again began to print letters supporting his position in his newspaper, especially to the readers who were particularly disturbed by Truett's claim that Hayden "never helped the mission work." On December 17 Hayden once again claimed that missionaries were starving while members of the Board were "paid in full." In the November 26 edition Hayden printed a letter from a certain Mr. Snodgrass, who blamed the entire controversy on B. H. Carroll. Snodgrass claimed: "Dr. Carroll may be more dogmatic than he thinks he is and naturally more vindictive than he would acknowledge if things do not go to suit him." Realizing that B. H. Carroll was taking a great deal of abuse from Hayden, Buckner, the president of the BGCT, wrote him a touching letter of confidence. Buckner stated that he knew that he was bearing the brunt of Hayden's diatribes, and that no matter the circumstance, he was behind him.[30] Prior to the Houston Convention, B. H. Carroll had asked for peace in the May 21 issue of the *Baptist Standard*, but his patience with Hayden had worn thin.

One of the most important events of the post-Houston Convention occurred in December 1896: M. D. Early resigned as Corresponding Secretary. Since this was such an important office, the Board realized that it must fill the position immediately. At the conclusion of an all-night prayer meeting at the First Baptist Church of Waco, J. B. Gambrell of Georgia was elected to the position with a salary of $1800.[31]

Gambrell, however, had incurred some debt and had a large family. The Board feared that Gambrell would not accept the position due to the meager salary. Five men decided to contribute funds to help supplement Gambrell's pay. Gambrell accepted the bonus, and when Hayden heard the plans he balked. In the February 11, 1897, edition of the *Texas Baptist and Herald* Hayden insisted that by giving Gambrell additional pay, these men had "disregarded constitutional authority" and the wishes of the messengers at Houston. Hayden also insisted that by accepting a bonus, Gambrell was downplaying the importance of the missionaries in the field. After all, the missionaries had received nothing extra. A week later on February 18, Hayden published an editorial in which he insisted that Gambrell turn over his supplement to the Convention for equal distribution among the missionaries. Hayden continued his attack on Gambrell in the March 11 issue of his newspaper. He believed the entire state should know of the "deceitful manner" in which this "Georgian" had attained his position. Despite Gambrell's claims that he attempted to be cordial with Hayden, Gambrell had made a dangerous enemy.[32]

This would not be the only time these men would disagree. Almost immediately upon his arrival in Texas, Gambrell began to promote the merits of the Convention system and the cooperative work in both the *Missionary Worker* and the *Baptist Standard*. The Convention plan is "based upon churches, which send messengers and contributions to a central body to plan and carry out Christian ministries beyond the local church. The convention usually covers a specific geographical area, as a county or state. Further, the convention may sponsor multiple ministries, limited only by its vision and resources, the same convention appointing different boards for foreign missions, home missions, Sunday School publications, Christian education, or whatever. . . In essence, this is a plan whereby cooperating churches work together."[33]

In these newspapers, Gambrell continually explained how denominational work must continue year round, and that these were effective models; that cooperation, a strong Board, and Convention were the keys to the entire system. Since every Baptist church is sovereign, Gambrell made sure that Baptists realized that the Convention model did not infringe on the autonomy of the local church. In the October 7 edition of the *Baptist Standard*, Gambrell claimed that "no church can exercise sovereignty in any such way as goes beyond its own sphere. Outside of that sphere it has no power and, in fact, no existence. The limitations of church sovereignty are the bounds of the church itself. All matters pertaining to more than one church are regulated by denominational polity."

Gambrell's position would be strengthened by letters and editorials that insinuated that Hayden and his faction were Gospel Mission Men. Also known as "Crawfordists" after their founder, T. P. Crawford, Gospel Missionaries believed that "missionaries should be sent directly by churches rather than a mission board. He [Crawford] also said that missionaries should receive no salaries beyond an initial grant to get them established, after which they should earn their own way."[34] In his 1892 book, *Churches to the Front!*, Crawford attacked the Southern Baptist Convention and its mission boards.[35] He was eventually dismissed by the Southern Baptist Convention's Foreign Mission Board.

Though Hayden had no ecclesiological relationship to Primitive Baptist Daniel Parker, Gambrell realized that he could use Hayden's arguments against the Executive Board to depict him as not only a Crawfordist, but also an advocate of Parker's radical doctrines. Parker had relocated from Illinois to the Nacogdoches area of east Texas in 1834. There he promoted his own unique doctrine known as "Two Seeds in the Spirit." This predestinarian doctrine stated that a person was elected by God as either a seed, and thus a child, of God or Satan. For this reason, he believed that mission boards, and any missionary endeavors for that matter, were useless since no one could write his or her own name in the "Lamb's Book of Life."

> Dear brethren, can you blame us for not believing the mission system now pursued, to be the way or medium through which the lord is about to fill the world with his gospel or preachers; when you are not able to show such or plan or society throughout the leads of the Bible. And I ask, can we believe that God ever designed so great a work to be performed in that way, and has given us no account in his word, so that his children might understand his will and agree in the work.[36]

In a manner similar to Parker, Gospel Missions advocates believed that there was no biblical precedent for mission boards. The Gospel Missions men, however, were for missions, but not by means of a mission board. Parker was against missions altogether. Hayden was also not against missions or mission boards. He was against certain members who he believed dominated the board, promoted nepotism, and wasted money. Hayden, therefore, was neither a Gospel Missions supporter nor a follower of Daniel Parker.

During the first half of the nineteenth century Parker's use of the Bible as a proof-text against mission societies dominated east Texas Baptist life.[37] Though this fear was still present in the 1890s, almost all east Texas Baptists were now missionary minded and many were in favor of the organized mission work. They did not want Parker's doctrines resurrected. Since the Gospel Mission Movement also based its anti-mission society position on a similar biblical argument, Gambrell was able to tap into the Baptist fear of its revival. If he could tie Hayden to the Gospel Missions movement and then by inference to Daniel Parker, Hayden would undoubtably lose a great deal of his support in east Texas.

Accusations that Hayden was a Gospel Missions man began to circulate almost immediately after the conclusion of the Houston Convention. Gambrell and the Board used this stigma to their advantage. In fact, in September 30 edition, B. H. Carroll called both Hayden and Burleson "Gospel Missions Men." Thus, their continual complaints and arguments were destroying the year-round work. During the ensuing years Gambrell and his cohorts further developed this theme and continued to pen editorials promoting the Board and Convention model while berating the Gospel Missions Men. As the 1897 Convention grew closer, Gambrell urged the readers of the *Baptist Standard* in the November 4 issue to go to the Convention and defeat the Haydenite faction, whose leadership Gambrell believed would "utterly fail to hold the working force of our people together."

Due to these pre-Convention charges, Hayden was immediately forced to deny his adherence to Crawfordism. Against these accusations, Hayden denied in the November 26 publication of the *Texas Baptist and Herald* that his followers were Gospel Missions Men, asking, "will anyone say that those who signed the Protest at Houston are opposed to Conventions?" A. J. Wharton wrote an editorial in Hayden's paper on July 29 asserting, "There are thousands of Baptists in Texas who are tinctured with the Crawford Movement in missions. Unless something is done at once to check the tide and nothing but retrenchment can do it, our mission work will be utterly ruined." In the September 2, 1897, edition of the *Texas Baptist and Herald*, Hayden continued his defense against Crawfordism by claiming that "if we wanted to build up Gospel Missions, so-called, distract and divide our people, and bury the well nigh already killed missions cause in Texas, we would seek to defeat the reform movement. To adopt reform unifies our people, to defeat it divides them." Returning to a familiar theme, the embattled journalist concluded: "The Churches of the State can never be united in mission work on a schedule of expenses in which four men, the secretary and the general missionaries, consume on their salaries and expenses a sum equal to the sum total of all the collections in the State, or a hundred percent of it."[38]

Hayden also often used letters from his readers to support his position, and for this reason these statements are significant. When asked directly by one of his readers what he thought of the Gospel Missions Movement, Hayden stated in the July 29, 1897, edition of the *Herald*: "I was always and always had been in favor of the organized work." In denying this charge, Hayden himself repudiated some of the more modern interpretations of his doctrine.[39] The Hayden Controversy, at its essence, was not primarily an ecclesiological struggle. Hayden never objected to centralization or to the Convention or the Board method itself, but rather to the body of men who composed the Board and ran the Convention year after year.

At the same time, Hayden did not help his cause by calling his followers the "Church Party" and his adversaries the "Board Party." In his book, *The Complete Conspiracy Trial*, Hayden clearly presented his position: "The Church Party claimed that the churches had a right to choose their own messengers and the Convention had no right to say to the churches which of their members they might and which they might not elect as their messengers; that if a Church should elect criminal, disreputable or immoral men as messengers to the Convention, the Convention provides, and refuse all her messengers. But the Convention could not discriminate, and say some of the messengers from a given church might be seated, and others not, except for adequate cause."[40]

During these years, Gambrell proved to be the leader in the Board's next decisions. He first delineated the merits of the Board and Convention. Against this positive example, in the July 4, 1889, edition of the *Missionary Worker* he offset advocates of the Gospel Missions Movement, who espoused the premise that "missionaries should be sent out only by local churches, not by mission boards . . . for a mission board to appoint, set salaries, and give directions for missionaries was tantamount to an episcopal function." While there may have been some individuals who supported the Gospel Missions Movement among Texas Baptists, the majority saw this stance as a serious danger to the missions cause.[41]

Ecclesiology, therefore, was only an ancillary part of the Hayden Controversy; it was used as weapon by the Board to rally Baptist support toward cooperative mission work and strengthen its position while the Convention was in session. If the Convention could pick and choose who could be recognized as messengers, Hayden could be removed with a simple majority. It was also used as a weapon by Hayden in his attempts to demonstrate how the Board chose to supersede biblical precedence and traditional Baptist ecclesiology. Sounding very much like a Crawfordist and realizing his seat at the Convention was at stake, Hayden stressed the traditional Baptist position that no entity held authority over the local church. In this respect, ecclesiology was part of the conflict, but not a major reason for its development.

Meanwhile, the Board of Trustees of Baylor University decided that the seventy-five-year-old president, R. C. Burleson, was due to retire.[42] In order to avoid the appearance of a compulsory termination, he was given the title of president emeritus. Burleson had not been perceived as incompetent, but was now, as J. M. Carroll stated, "growing old and feeble."[43] In a moving letter to the Board of Trustees of Baylor University, Burleson made clear that he did not agree with the action; but at the same time, he loved Baylor and reluctantly vowed to do whatever was required to help the school prepare for the twentieth century.

While Burleson's defense of Hayden made him an adversary of B. H. Carroll, chairman of the Baylor Board of Trustees, the elderly president had other troubles as well. William Cowper Brann had moved to Waco in 1894, and began to publish his periodical, *The Iconoclast*, the following year. Realizing that controversy sold magazines, Brann moved into this Baptist haven and began to unleash editorials against Baylor University and the Baptist denomination in general, and especially those in Waco.

Brann had several encounters with the Baptists in Waco and Baylor University over their overt anti-Catholicism, false claims of miraculous elixirs in the *Baptist Standard*, and desire to save the world from the Catholic menace when downtown Waco was infested with prostitutes, saloons, and frequent gunfights.[44] Many Baptists in Waco were incensed with Brann. Even though he began to receive death threats, he was not deterred from attacking the Baptist denomination on every front. These events proved minor and were just a precursor to his upcoming attack on Baylor University.

Brann's attack on Baylor University, and Rufus Burleson in particular, was over the unexpected pregnancy of a Brazilian Baylor student named Antonia Teixeira. When she was twelve years old, Antonia was sent to Baylor University by foreign missionary Z. C. Taylor to receive a Baptist education. Since she had no money, she was permitted to live in Burleson's home where she helped Mrs. Burleson in the kitchen in exchange for tuition, room, and board. Antonia was not the only boarder in the Burleson home. The brother of Dr. Burleson's son-in-law and editor of the Baptist magazine *The Guardian*, Steven Morris, was also living in their home.[45]

Antonia claimed that Morris drugged and attacked her on three different occasions. She reported the incident to Mrs. Burleson, but no one took her word over that of Morris. Rufus Burleson denied that his wife had any knowledge of the event and that the girl was "utterly untrustworthy and that she was crazy after boys."[46] Brann wasted little time in calling Burleson and Baylor University to task over their treatment of this girl who had been placed in their custody for education, religious training, and safekeeping. Brann immediately fired off an editorial in the July 1895 edition of *The Iconoclast*: "What did the aged president of Baylor, that sanctum sanctorum of the Baptist church, do about it? Did he assist in bringing to justice the man who dared invade the sanctity of his household. . .? Not exactly. He rushed into print with a statement to the effect that the child was a thief and 'crazy after the boys.'"[47]

Morris was brought to trial for rape, but the case was dismissed because of a hung jury. No further charges were levied against him, and Baylor advocates hoped the incident would disappear. Brann, however, continued to attack Baylor University and the Baptists of Waco at every possible instance. The situation became so acute that, according to Baylor legend, on October 2, 1897, several Baylor students kidnapped Brann and, if not for the interference of some conscientious Baylor faculty, might have hung him. Brann was later involved in two shootouts with his Baptist enemies on the streets of Waco. In the first episode, Brann was attacked and managed to kill his two assailants. On the second occasion, Brann shot and killed his attacker, the father of a Baylor student, but he also lost his life in the exchange of gunfire.

Because Burleson had sided with Hayden against the direction of the BGCT Executive Board and handled the Brann situation poorly, he came under attack from several of his former supporters. Burleson had outlived his usefulness and was no longer an asset to Baylor University and the ever-growing anti-Haydenite faction. Moreover, it was no secret that B. H. Carroll coveted the presidency of Baylor. Of course, Brann picked up on Carroll's motive, stating: "I greatly regret that my Baptist brethren . . . should have gotten into a spiteful and un-Christian snarl over so pitiful thing as Baylor's $2000 presidency—that they should give to the world such a flagrant imitation of a lot of cut-throat degenerates out for the long green."[48]

B. H. Carroll wasted little time in launching scathing remarks against Burleson. Carroll declared in the September 23, 1897, publication of the *Baptist Standard* that Burleson was "An old man, 74 years old, who has held office for forty-six consecutive years, and failed of lawful election, seeks to be unlawfully restored and forced upon a school whose Trustees, Faculty, and Students do not want him." In response, Hayden used the popularity of Burleson and his forced retirement as a weapon to strike against B. H. Carroll and the Board. Before long, Hayden had fashioned Burleson into a martyr.

The chain of events that led up to the 1897 BGCT were still not over. The 1897 regular session of the BGCT was originally scheduled to be held in the small north Texas town of Weatherford. Hayden, who was very popular in north Texas, expected a large "Church Party" turnout due to the locale.

Hayden's adversaries were concerned. In a letter to B. H. Carroll, George W. Baines warned that "Hayden is now marshaling his forces" for the Weatherford BGCT.[49] While preparations were being made at Weatherford, the Board, represented by B. H. Carroll, informed the town's citizenry that it could expect up to 2000 messengers and should be prepared to feed and house them. This was not an uncommon practice. The city where the Convention was held was expected to serve as a host to the visiting messengers. Hayden, however, claimed that Carroll delivered this message to scare the town with these great demands. According to A. S. Bunting, Hayden then offered Weatherford 100 tents, 800 cots, and $1200 to feed the messengers if they would stand firm and still hold the session in their city.[50] Evidently the town realized it could not host this many people and asked that the Convention be relocated.[51]

Even before B. H. Carroll's visit to Weatherford, Hayden foresaw what was about to happen. In the August 26 edition of the *Herald* he stated, "Now we have it from a strictly reliable source that the leaders in the Board are trying to carry the Convention as far from North Texas, and to locate it as far South of Waco as practical, and that Temple is the place under consideration." He was correct. Temple was the new site chosen for the event. As soon as Temple had been announced as the new locale, however, a yellow fever scare swept through the city. Hayden rallied his readers, encouraging them to "pay no attention to the Yellow Fever scare." He was attempting to secure a train so his advocates, especially those from the north Texas area, could reach Temple in force. Nonetheless, due to the yellow fever scare, the 1897 BGCT was moved to San Antonio, a town that was even farther south.[52] As he left for the Convention, Hayden was enthusiastic, but sensed that the odds for success were not in his favor.

Both factions seemed indefatigable in their efforts to debase the other and gather as many messengers to their respective causes at the Convention as they could. Hayden's attacks on the Board had been consistent and more vitriolic than before. In the October 21, 1897, edition of the *Texas Baptist and Herald*, Hayden stated that "it would be an endless job to correct all the mistakes that Dr. Cranfill has published in his Standard in regard to myself." The Board brought in their warrior, J. B. Gambrell, whom they hoped would lead the charge against Hayden. In this regard, J. M. Carroll stated, "First in order of importance was the coming to Texas of J. B. Gambrell. Few events have meant more to Texas Baptists and their interests than the coming of this American commoner. He came at the right time. He exactly fitted into a great situation." Two days before the Convention was to begin on November 5, the advocates of the Board held an informal caucus at the old Menger Hotel in downtown San Antonio. They had been denied satisfaction by failing to unseat Hayden at Houston, but they were going to be better prepared for this Convention.

Hayden had received word of the scheduled meeting and knew the purpose. The "Maverick Caucus," as he dubbed it in the November 11 edition of the *Herald*, was designed to secure "the appointment of Board members and their friends at the very outset of the tribunal."

The Board constituents would later deny that these meetings were designed to oust Hayden, but the *Texas Baptist and Herald* was the main topic of conversation.[53]

The 1897 Convention began on November 5. At the outset, business was conducted as usual. R. C. Buckner was elected president and the regular Board officers assumed their positions of leadership. Convention messengers received a telegram from B. H. Carroll saying that his wife was dying. Truett led a prayer for the restoration of her health, but the next day she died.[54] Due to the death of Mrs. Carroll and his own illness, B. H. Carroll missed the Convention.

R. C. Buckner appointed a seven-man credential committee to review the seat of any member against whom a protest was lodged. The committee was comprised of J. M. Robertson, G. W. Baines, J. C. Gentry, R. A. Lee, Bennett Hatcher, J. C. Burkett, and I. B. Kimbrough. Robertson excused himself and L. R. Millican took his place. Due to the strenuous work ahead of them, three more men, S. J. Anderson, W. H. Parks, and J. H. Roberts, were added to the committee. Also important is the fact that several individual messengers were questioned as to their status.

One of Hayden's adversaries, L. M. Mays, then levied five reasons to remove Hayden from the Convention:

> First, he has violated the spirit and letter of the constitution of this body which says
> The object of this Convention shall be missionary and educational, the promotion of harmony of feeling and concert of action among Baptists, and a system of operative measures for the promotions of the interests of the Redeemer's Kingdom. This fundamental law, he has violated by a ceaseless and hurtful war upon the plans, policies, work and workers of this Convention.
> Second, he is and has been in open and notorious opposition to the convention and its mandates.
> Third, because he will not abide and support the findings and decisions of this Convention, its plans and policies, for organized and co-operative work, and has announced that he will

> not in the future abide by its decisions, unless they be settled his way.
>
> Fourth, he is unworthy of a seat in this Convention on moral grounds. He has assailed the public and private character of the Superintendent of Missions and the Board of Directors by falsely accusing them of dishonorable practices in the misuse of mission money.
>
> Fifth, that said course of conduct has been pursued by him for such a length of time, and with such continuous and persistent malice and traduction toward the Convention ... in spite of repeated admonitions and mandates of the Convention, as to render his connection with it a standing menace to the life of the whole body.[55]

A majority of the Credentials Committee recommended that he be "unseated." The Convention then gave Hayden "forty-five minutes in which to defend himself" and appointed W. H. Jenkins to reply to Hayden's response. A vote to act upon the Committee's recommendation was to be taken immediately after their speeches. The plan unfolded as outlined and the vote was taken. Hayden lost his seat as a Convention messenger by a 582 to 104 count.[56]

Hayden's unseating was not surprising. The anti-Haydenite faction's victory may be attributed to four things: Gambrell's articles depicting the merits of the Convention and Board model, Hayden's inability to remove himself from the stigma of the Gospel Missions Movement, the relocation of the Convention to San Antonio, and the organizational efforts achieved at the Maverick Caucus. While the Board Party had been inadequately prepared for the Houston Convention in 1896, the opposite proved to be true for the San Antonio Convention of 1897.

Immediately after the Convention, Hayden began to fire editorials at the Board Party. Hayden claimed in the November 11 edition that "the Reformers of the church party are a discriminating power. They are clear in thought and constant in views. The Board Party are confused in the ideas and inconsistent in utterances." In the same issue he reiterated, "The Church Party denies that the Convention is sovereign, but subordinate to the church, as a joint committee of all the churches. Read Matthew 16:18." The Board advocates believed that they had achieved complete victory in the unseating of Hayden. The 1897 BGCT had demonstrated to the Baptists of Texas that the Convention model had won and Hayden's influence had waned. An editorial in the November 18 *Baptist Standard* made this clear: "The Baptist in Texas who now raises a hand to fight Dr. Hayden will be under the suspicion of making war on the dead." It seemed Texas Baptists could expect a more cordial Convention the next year at Waco.

Even though the anti-Haydenite faction claimed that Hayden's influence "was dead," it feared that his spirit would be resurrected at the next Convention. Gambrell and the Board Party continued to publish articles against the Gospel Missions Movement, all the while suggesting that the editor of the *Texas Baptist and Herald*, or anyone who was against the Convention method, was its advocate. In the July 15, 1897, edition of the *Baptist Standard*, Gambrell lambasted the Crawfordists of Texas when he stated that "these brethren are spending their time trying to pull our mission work to pieces. They are not going to the inactive churches, but to the active. They have the spirit of distraction and God is not pleased with their spirit. Wherever the spirit of fault finding and strife is found, their spiritual leanness is found. Churches and pastors are fruitless. The thing is not of God." Articles against extreme Landmarkism were also published in the June 23, 1898, issue of the *Baptist Standard*. Due to the intense nature of the newspaper war, Gambrell published another article on March 24, 1898, encouraging his readers not to become discouraged with *The Baptist Standard*; the paper existed solely to serve the denomination. At the same time, Gambrell claimed in the October 1 issue of the *Missionary Worker* that nothing could be trusted that was found in the pages of the *Texas Baptist and Herald*.

After such a resounding defeat at the San Antonio Convention, one might think that Hayden would have taken a lower profile for a time. But quite the opposite was true, and on April 28, 1898, Hayden escalated the controversy to an unprecedented level. He took the Convention's decision to unseat him as a messenger to a court of law and sued some thirty men he believed to be responsible for his unseating. The most notable plaintiffs included J. B. Cranfill, J. B. Gambrell, G. W. Truett, W. H. Jenkins, J. M. Carroll, B. H. Carroll, and R. T. Hanks. R. C. Buckner was never among those being sued, even though he held the presidency of the BGCT for twenty years. Buckner's absence from the lawsuit may be due to his lack of participation in the newspaper war. Buckner was always more concerned with the orphanage than denominational politics and published his own orphanage reports annually. Hayden's intention was to regain his status as a valid messenger.

Hayden insisted that this unparalleled action was necessary, since he had done everything within regular Baptist polity to remedy his disenfranchisement, but had been denied satisfaction by a conspiracy of Convention leaders at San Antonio.[57] Therefore, he claimed that he had no other choice but to take the matter to court. Hayden called this episode the "Conspiracy Trial."

At first, those thirty persons named in the $100,000 suit did not take the matter seriously. Soon, however, they came to realize that the trial would be long and costly. The court battles lasted for seven years. When the legal affairs ended in 1905, there had been four separate trials, each one played out in the *Texas Baptist and Herald*, and all under Judge Richard Morgan, whom the defendants believed had openly sided with Hayden.[58]

Meanwhile, Hayden escalated the situation even further by distributing a special edition of the *Texas Baptist and Herald* at the meeting of the Southern Baptist Convention at Norfolk, Virginia. In this special edition issued on April 28, 1898, Hayden put forth his side of the story, placing special emphasis on his reform effort, the salaries of the Board, the actions of the Houston Convention, the tactics that had led to the removal of the BGCT from Weatherford to San Antonio, and his disenfranchisement at San Antonio. Hayden believed that these affairs deserved a larger forum; however, his actions only deepened the resolve of his opponents. Not only did Baptists in Texas know of the BGCT's problems, but now the entire Southern Baptist Convention was made privy to Texas' internecine affairs. Realizing that Hayden was not finished, the leaders of the Convention rallied their supporters to ensure that they would register as messengers at the Waco Convention should further action against Hayden be necessary again.

Old Baylor University at Independence, ca. 1860 (reproduction courtesy of Texas Collection, Baylor University)

Once part of the woman's dormitory, these four pillars are all that remain of Baylor University at Independence. (reproduction courtesy of Texas Collection, Baylor University)

A young Benajah Harvey Carroll while pastor of the First Baptist Church of Waco, ca. 1885 (reproduction courtesy of Texas Collection, Baylor University)

Samuel Augustus Hayden after the Civil War, ca. 1875 (reproduction courtesy of Texas Collection, Baylor University)

Baylor University at Independence, date unknown (reproduction courtesy of the Texas Collection, Baylor University)

The Carroll brothers in their youth, ca. 1880, J. M. Carroll standing and B. H. Carroll sitting (reproduction courtesy of Southwestern Baptist Theological Seminary)

Dr. J. B. Cranfill, the man who suffered Hayden's harshest editorial attacks, ca. 1917 (reproduction courtesy of Southwestern Baptist Theological Seminary)

James Burton Gambrell, ca 1900. His arrival in Texas signaled the end of Hayden's bid for power in the Baptist General Convention of Texas. (reproduction courtesy of the Texas Collection, Baylor University)

The most famous picture of B. H. Carroll, ca 1906. Notice the long beard, which was a trademark of Landmarkists. (reproduction courtesy of Texas Collection, Baylor University)

Rufus Columbus Burleson late in his presidency at Baylor University, ca. 1894 (reproduction courtesy of Texas Collection, Baylor University)

George Washington Truett, ca. 1916, pastor of First Baptist Dallas and the man who helped remove S. A. Hayden from the 1897 Baptist General Convention of Texas (reproduction courtesy of Texas Collection, Baylor University)

One of the few existing photographs of Samuel Augustus Hayden, ca. 1918 (reproduction courtesy of Southwestern Baptist Theological Seminary)

CHAPTER 7

THE END OF AN ERA

EVEN IN THE MIDST of Hayden's litigation and incessant diatribes, the Board believed another victory was within its grasp. Several favorable elements combined as the Convention was called to order. The 1898 regular session of the BGCT took place at Waco, a city known for its support of the Board and its anti-Hayden sentiment. In addition, Hayden's dissemination of his vitriolic special edition of the *Texas Baptist and Herald* at the Southern Baptist Convention had embarrassed Texas Baptists before their nationwide brethren.[1] Most importantly, there was now a precedent to remove a messenger from the Convention for being a sower of discord. It would prove to be much easier to uphold this ruling a second time than to enforce it the first. Hayden had little chance of regaining his seat at the Waco Convention.

The session began as usual with prayer, a devotional, and a sermon. Then the Convention's attention turned to the Committee on Credentials. Four challenges to messenger status were placed before the Convention, which then acted as its own Credentials Committee. Three of the challenges were against specific churches, and the other was against Hayden.

President Buckner then made a "historic ruling"[2] from the chair that further articulated Baptist polity regarding messenger status. He "ruled out of order the challenges against the churches upon the ground that the Convention is composed of individual messengers and not of churches, claiming no ecclesiastical power, but recognizing the absolute independence of the churches." Since the messengers themselves had not been challenged, they were allowed to be seated. This ruling left only one matter to be dealt with: Hayden.

But before turning to Hayden, the Convention elected officers. The Convention again elected Buckner president, and A. E. Baten and J. H. Truett were secretaries. The same slate of officers had been witness to Hayden's dismissal in 1897, would be once again in the constant view of the 2,494 Convention messengers endorsing the precedent set just a year earlier. Thus, even when Hayden was permitted to speak, there were always present on the stage those who stood against him and his policies. Immediately following the election of officers, Hayden's adversaries moved against him.

O. S. Parks, a messenger from the Pecos Church, officially moved to deny Hayden a seat in the Convention once again. Each charge was read by J. M. Robertson, followed by proof texts by G. W. Truett, most of which was compiled from selections from the pages of the *Texas Baptist and Herald.* The most damning of these denunciations included his unwarranted attacks on the Convention, his continued claims that several corresponding secretaries had falsified their records, his assertions that the Board functioned as an episcopate, the unproven claims that the Board falsified the mission reports, the portrayal of the Corresponding Secretary as the Roman pontiff, and his distribution of a special edition of the *Texas Baptist and Herald* at the Southern Baptist Convention, which contained articles that were based on acrimonious innuendos.[3]

The Convention gave Hayden thirty minutes to respond. Three themes were prominent: his independent right as an editor to publish freely; his desire to reform the Convention; and the sovereign church's right to seat its own messenger. J. M. Robertson was given an additional twenty minutes to reply. He merely stated that the accusations leveled against Hayden were true and that for the good of Baptist life in Texas, Hayden must be denied a seat. The vote was taken, and Hayden was overwhelmingly defeated by a 2,300 to 200 count.[4]

Not surprised by his resounding defeat, Hayden nevertheless remained undaunted. He knew that the next Convention was to be held in his own territory of influence: Dallas. Hayden believed he would finally have a fair chance to regain his seat and receive some manner of compensation.

Throughout the remainder of 1898 and well into 1899, both sides in the dispute attempted to buttress the merits of their own systems and debase the efforts of the other. Gambrell continued his efforts to educate Texas Baptists as to exactly what the BGCT leadership was trying to do. He claimed that the purpose of the BGCT and its Board was to have a deliberative body intact year round so that mission funds could be continually disbursed wherever and whenever needed. Furthermore, he believed that by working cooperatively through Boards rather than individual churches, missionaries would be dispersed more properly rather than being concentrated in one area of the state. He further explained that the Board had no control over the local church and received no salary for its services. Advancing this platform, he and his coworkers labored so hard to garner as many delegates as possible in Dallas that Hayden claimed that: "No higher evidence of the Board Parties [*sic*] estimate of the strength of the Church Party could be given than by the fact that they have employed the bulk of the mission money in employment of men to 'line up' the churches. Scarcely one particle of genuine missionary work is being done in Texas."[5]

Hayden had good reason to boast. Many of the largest associations in the Dallas region were penning letters to the *Texas Baptist and Herald* pledging their support. Hayden was always grateful for their support of the sovereign church policy. He was especially pleased that the large New Bethlehem, Ellis, and Dallas associations had endorsed his efforts. Hayden now began to protest the money-based system for determining the number of messengers a church was allowed to send to the Convention each year. He especially disliked Article II, section II of the BGCT constitution, which read: "Each Church shall be entitled to two messengers, one additional messenger for each $25 dollar contributed to the funds of the Convention, and in no case shall any one

Church be entitled to more than eight messengers."[6] Hayden asserted in the October 26, 1898, edition of the *Texas Baptist and Herald* that a money-based membership was unfair to poorer churches that wanted to participate in the BGCT.

Attempting to help his old friend, R. C. Burleson pled in the October 26, 1898, edition of the *Herald* for strong attendance at Dallas or "our beloved Zion will be put back at least twenty years." E. B. Hardie, also a strong Haydenite, even wrote Buckner a letter accusing him of failing to lend support to Hayden's position, which Hardie believed he held in his heart, out of a fear of damaging fiscal gifts to the orphanage. Hardie reminded Buckner that Saul had to stand up to Barnabas, and that Saul's ministry was blessed because of it.[7] He too must make his stand for the truth. Hayden ended his final push with a scathing editorial on Gambrell on November 9, whom he likened to a mercenary.

Gambrell remained calm, however. He believed many of the country churches, which claimed to support Hayden, would splinter during the session.[8] In an attempt to harden the position against Hayden, Gambrell published his version of the previous year's events and reiterated Hayden's destructive role in BGCT ventures in the September 1, 1899, issue of the *Missionary Worker*. Once again he rallied support of the Board to register for the Dallas Convention in October. B. H. Carroll also urged a large turnout. Unlike at the previous San Antonio and Waco conventions, BGCT leaders were unsure of the outcome in Dallas.

Tensions filled the air as the Board and the Church parties registered their advocates at Dallas.[9] Both sides must have realized that this Convention would be a decisive event in the controversy. If Hayden could not win in Dallas, it would be unlikely that he could win in any other city. On November 10 the fourteenth annual session of the Baptist General Convention of Texas was called to order at the Great Music Hall Auditorium of the Texas State Fair Association in Dallas.[10]

When all of the eligible delegates were seated, it was announced that 2,494 messengers had registered to support the issues at hand. Buckner was once more elected president with E. A. Baten and F. M. McConnell serving as the secretaries. This election was the first blow against the Church Party, which had run candidates against the three men, as well as against J. B. Gambrell for his position as Corresponding Secretary. Each had been defeated by almost a two to one ratio.

A Credentials Committee was elected. After a brief deliberation, the Credentials Committee presented those individuals whose seats had been challenged before the body. There were five different challenges presented that day. In a surprising twist, B. H. Carroll, R. C. Buckner, and J. B. Gambrell's seats had been challenged.[11] This action led to serious arguments on the floor. R. T. Hanks immediately challenged the opposition to Buckner, and his objection was sustained.[12] In quick succession, the challenges to Gambrell and Carroll were also overturned. The Convention turned to the remainder of the individuals who had been challenged, particularly S. A. Hayden. A motion was made calling for all objections to be sustained. This motion was rejected by the body by a 1,763 to 648 count. This action was the second blow against Hayden. By this time the messengers realized that the editor of the *Texas Baptist and Herald* was once again outnumbered. His fate again rested alone on the judgement of the Credentials Committee.

At this time, an argument was raised that the original Credentials Committee was biased since no Church Party advocates had been selected to serve on it. However, it was determined that this motion was out of order since the BGCT did not recognize any such group. This was a third blow to Hayden's cause. A second Credentials Committee was chosen to focus upon the official charges against those individuals who had not been sustained. Though other individuals were being investigated, the Convention's concern was squarely focused on Hayden. After deliberations, W. M. Harris presented for the Committee its decision concerning Hayden:

> Your committee on challenges beg leave to submit the following report in reference to the challenge against S. A. Hayden: Since said challenge is based upon the ground that the said S. A. Hayden is constantly at war upon the work of the Convention, thereby violating the constitution of the Convention; and, since the constitution of the Convention, Article I, Sec-

> tion 2, declares it to be a part of the objects of this Convention to promote harmony of feeling and concert of action among Baptists, and a system of operative measures for the promotion of the interests of the redeemer's Kingdom, your committee recommends that the challenge be sustained, your committee taking cognizance of the policy of the said S. A. Hayden's paper, *The Texas Baptist and Herald*.[13]

The Committee on Credentials granted Hayden twenty minutes to reply to the charges. Hayden's reply was caustic. He claimed that his accusers were themselves plaintiffs in a civil trial and thus could not be trusted. Cranfill, who was on the stage and but a few feet behind Hayden, remained stoic throughout the response, despite taking the brunt of Hayden's wrath. W. B. Denson then spoke for the Committee. He merely reiterated that the Committee had found the charges to be true. Ballots were then distributed to the messengers. The final tally stood 557 in favor of seating Hayden and 1181 desiring not to seat Hayden.[14] Even in his geographical stronghold, Hayden had again been denied a seat.

The Convention, however, was not finished with Hayden. For the last several years valuable Convention time had been spent quarreling with Hayden.[15] The majority of the messengers were tired of his antics. A resolution was adopted which the Convention majority believed would end this affair once and for all. The resolution stated:

> Article IX.—Whenever any church or association or society shall by a majority vote of the Convention be declared to be in an attitude of general or continued hostility or unfriendliness to the work or purposes of the Convention, or when any person is declared to be in such attitude, then such church or association or society, shall, by such majority vote, be denied the privilege of sending messengers to the Convention, and such person shall, by such a vote, be denied a seat as a messenger from any church, association or society, and when such church association or society shall be denied messengers, or such person denied a seat as a messenger, then the privilege so

> denied shall not thereafter be exercised by said church, association or society or person, until granted by a majority vote of the Convention after permanent organization.[16]

This resolution made it clear to Hayden and his advocates that the editor would never regain his seat at the BGCT.[17] Several of Hayden's most ardent adherents immediately left the Music Hall and convened at another location.[18] After a brief discussion there, they decided to form a new convention.[19] Hayden, however, was against such a move, apparently still believing that the BGCT should be reformed rather than abandoned.[20]

The *Baptist Standard* of November 16 immediately proclaimed the victory of the Convention over this troublesome minority. With a headline reading: "A World Beater: The Greatest Baptist Convention That Ever Met," initial gloating seemed rampant. One editorial in the November 23 edition of the *Standard* stated that "[T]he disorganizers were out in force. They had published far and wide that if the Board would place the Convention at Dallas, which was accessible for all, they would have a large majority at the Convention; would send Dr. Gambrell back to Georgia, take charge of the schools [*sic*] property of the state, and in general revolutionize the Baptist work in Texas." In sarcastic detail, the article explained how each of these events failed. Hayden's only reply was to blame his defeat on a conspiracy conjured up by his old nemesis, R. T. Hanks. In the November 30, 1898, edition of the *Texas Baptist and Herald*, Hayden proclaimed that "the historic Hanks sat by the President during the entire Convention and largely directed him in the proceedings of the Convention."

The 1899 Convention, however, was not the last time that Hayden made an appearance at the BGCT. Hayden made one last attempt to regain his seat at the 1900 regular session of the BGCT, held again at Waco. There he was arraigned and a vote was taken in order to determine whether he could be registered as a legal messenger. He received only two votes,[21] and those belonged to Hayden and his son.[22] Obviously the Haydenites realized that there was no point in registering as messengers to the BGCT Conventions as their cause was lost. Contrary to Hayden's leanings, they were desirous of a new organization.

In fact, they had already begun to take steps in that direction.

As evidenced by their turnout at the 1900 BGCT, Hayden's advocates had spurned the BGCT action. Just a few months earlier on July 6 the dissenters had met at Troupe, Texas, and formed the East Texas Baptist Convention and approved a constitution.[23] This Haydenite group changed its name to the Baptist Missionary Association in December of 1900.[24] Only forty-five churches were represented. This low turnout led J. B. Gambrell to proclaim in the February 15, 1900, edition of the *Missionary Worker* that the East Baptist Convention would never succeed.

However, when word spread that a group had left the BGCT, Baptist churches from all over the state wanted to affiliate with the new association in protest of the BGCT's heavy-handed actions. In particular, the churches in the Dallas Association claimed to have joined the BMA because they did not approve of the way the BGCT was handling its missionary work and held in disdain Hayden's disenfranchisement. At Jack's Creek on August 7, 1901, the BMA held its first annual meeting with more than 2,000 messengers seated. In comparison, the BGCT registered only 1,672 messengers. These numbers suggest that in the early twentieth century, the BMA posed a serious threat to BGCT dominance.

The BMA believed that its reasons for separation from the BGCT were justified. R. C. Vance, a historian of the Baptist Missionary Association, cites several of the early incidents that promoted discontent, particularly the mysterious disappearance of Cranfill's records and J. M. Carroll's salary. Hayden's attempts at reform had reinforced a desire by the Board Party to remove him from their midst. This action finally occurred in 1897; however, the final straw to force the schism was the addition of Article Nine at the 1899 Convention. Vance stated that a new Convention was needed because Article Nine "drove the wedge of division deeper between the two factions existing among the Baptists of Texas. The Convention now had legal rights to bind the churches and to refuse them an opportunity to speak their views."[25] W. H. Parks, a pastor and contemporary BMA historian, continued along the same vein when he stated: "Have the Baptists of Texas gone boldly into Rome, that there is crime in criticizing public men and public measures, that they would bridle free speech, that they would muzzle an independent press?"[26]

Both factions delineated the rationale for the final division of Texas Baptists differently. On the one hand, Vance believed that all these prior events led up to three foundational arguments for separation:

> (1) The money basis of representation which made it possible for the rich church to send more messengers to the annual meeting thereby controlling the sessions.
> (2) The Ninth Article to the Constitution which enabled the Convention to refuse a messenger from a church and yet receive other messengers from the same church if the body so desired. In the opinion of the leaders of the Association this caused the Baptist General Convention to become an Episcopal body.
> (3) The taking of the Rusk Academy away from the Cherokee Baptist Association, without the consent and over the protest and vote of the Cherokee Baptist Association. This one thing with regard to the Rusk Academy caused twenty-nine churches to send messengers to Troupe, Texas, to organize the East Texas Convention in July of 1900.[27]

Furthermore, Vance argued that the BMA did not separate from the BGCT because it did not agree with the Convention-Board System or the cooperative mission work. In fact, the original constitution of the East Texas Baptist Convention, which was adopted by the BMA, is quite similar to that of the BGCT. There was nothing the new Convention could do about the Rusk Academy, but the other problems were corrected. Article Three Section One stated that "[T]he messengers holding the sessions of this convention shall be CHOSEN BY their respective churches which they represent." Article Three Section Four states that "[E]ach church admitted to this convention shall be entitled to two messengers and in the event that a church has 200 or more members it shall have three messengers."

Hence, the BMA was not against the BGCT Board/Convention structure, but rather the domination of some of its perpetual Board members. In spite of the above, the BMA would also choose to elect an Executive Board that was in charge of the distribution of all funds. This in itself destroys the premise that the Haydenites were advocates of the Gospel Missions Movement. If the Haydenites had been Gospel Missions Men, they would never have chosen to work through a centralized Convention and Board. Specifically, advocates of the Gospel Missions Movement rejected any use of boards in missionary endeavors.

The BMA's Constitution also demonstrated its desire to make each church's voice equal at the Convention. This is the rationale behind the refusal to allow churches to purchase extra seats at the Convention. Hayden and his adherents had long believed that this polity showed favoritism to churches that had more money, but not necessarily a large membership. Thus, in the BMA's Constitution, each church with more than two hundred members, regardless of its fiscal status, was entitled to a third messenger.

In addition, the historic definition of Belton in 1895, when coupled with the BGCT's adoption of Article Nine, allowed the Convention to deny a seat to a messenger from a church where the other messengers from the same church may have already been seated. Who was to be sovereign in the messenger approval process, the church or the Convention? The BGCT believed it was the Convention, while the BMA maintained that the power rested in the individual church. Both groups held Landmark ideas, but the BMA maintained the sovereign church principle to a greater degree. For this reason, the BMA has traditionally been perceived as extreme Landmarkists or Crawfordists, while the BGCT had escaped this stigma because of each group's differences over this one point. Despite their aversion to BGCT Board dominance, the BMA Constitution placed no restraints on the number of terms a person could serve on a Board. However, every word uttered at a Board meeting was to be published in the denominational newspaper, thereby allowing all the faithful to be privy to the Board's actions.[28]

Ecclesiology has its place in the Hayden Controversy, but this ecclesiological point is minuscule when compared to the accumulation of events that had transpired since at least 1877. The ecclesiological argument purported by the Board, therefore, was merely a means to secure votes against Hayden and end his annual tirades. If J. B. Gambrell and his adherents had not felt compelled to label the Haydenites as extremist Landmarkists or Gospel Missionists, the 1899 Dallas vote might have been quite different. Though many of the messengers to this Convention may have believed in the sovereign church, the fear that Hayden might be a Crawfordist may have pushed them to the Board's side. Although this may have been an unprincipled strategy, Gambrell's ploy proved successful. Hayden was defeated, and, apparently, Gambrell believed that the end justified the means.

Furthermore, the Haydenites resisted the manner in which the Board attempted to stifle both the *Texas Baptist and Herald* and anyone else who disagreed with its policies. The BMA maintained that, from the beginning, Baptists always believed in the principle of freedom of speech; therefore, Article Nine had all but destroyed this sacred tenet. In Article Five of the East Texas Baptist-BMA Constitution, freedom of speech and the right to disagree with each other were upheld.[29]

By 1905 the number of delegates to the BMA had drastically dropped, and only 321 churches were represented while the BGCT registered 490 churches. The BMA's numbers continued to diminish in 1906 and 1907, primarily due to the internal squabbles resulting from the BMA's close affiliation with the radical Landmarkism of the Ben Bogard Movement in Arkansas. Bogard was an anti-Board leader in Arkansas who launched his movement while the Hayden Controversy was raging in Texas. Unlike Hayden, Bogard was a true Gospel Missions advocate. He espoused radical Landmarkist ideas, despised the office of Corresponding Secretary of Missions, and even demanded that the Southern Baptist Convention move away from Mission Boards or his organization would leave the SBC. The SBC did not acquiesce and Bogard's followers formed their own General Association in 1905. Despite the General Association's fear of domination, Bogard was the autocrat of the organization.[30]

Hayden's alignment with Bogard may have repelled many of the initial BMA members who were upset with the domination of certain BGCT Board members, but who were unwilling to become radical Landmarkists. Historian W. W. Barnes suggests that Bogard was indeed a genuine advocate of the Gospel Missions Movement.[31] In fact, in 1905, the same year BMA's numbers began to decline, Bogard made his threat to take his followers and leave the Southern Baptist Convention. Those Texas Baptists who had joined the BMA were angry at the BGCT, not necessarily the SBC. Thus, of the original BMA constituency, no doubt the less ecclesiastically troublesome members returned to the more stable BGCT over time.

On the other hand, the BGCT had accomplished its goal by passing Article Nine. Neither Hayden nor any other disgruntled personality could disrupt the proceedings of the Convention in the same way again. B. F. Riley suggested that the break was "the direct outgrowth of the action of the Convention in declining seats in the body to certain members who were opposed to the State Convention."[32] After the decisive victory at Dallas, J. B. Gambrell challenged Hayden publicly in the February 15, 1899, publication of the *Missionary Worker* to admit that he was a Gospel Missions Man. Despite his earlier denials, Hayden made no direct answer to Gambrell.

With the birth of the BMA, Texas now had two state conventions. Hayden's paper now supported the new body, while it still continued to cast doubt upon the work of the BGCT. The *Baptist Standard* maintained its support of the BGCT ventures, which continued to thrive. Though separated, both groups appeared to be making progress and a peace seemed to fall upon the Texas Baptists. It seemed that the Hayden Controversy, which had dominated Baptist affairs for so long, was drawing to a close. However, there would be one final event.

Hayden's affiliation with the BMA took him increasingly out of the circles of the BGCT statewide work, even though the *Texas Baptist and Herald* continued to question the policies of the BGCT. The statewide aspects of the Hayden Controversy were all but over by 1901. Yet, in May 1904 Hayden and Cranfill, who happened to be on the same train bound for the Southern Baptist Convention in Nashville, had one last dramatic encounter.

Somewhere in the vicinity of Texarkana, Arkansas, Hayden and Cranfill were surprised to find themselves alone in the same train washroom. Cranfill pulled a gun from his toiletry bag and fired two rounds in the general direction of Hayden. Miraculously, neither man was hit by either of the shots. As had been the case during their quarrels in the 1890s, each man interpreted the event differently.

Cranfill sought to deal with the incident as discreetly as possible. In a letter to the First Baptist Church of Dallas, in which he offered to rescind his ministerial credentials over the affair, he outlined the details of the encounter. Cranfill claimed that while he was preparing to enter the washroom, he found a pistol that his son had placed in his bag. As his toiletries were in the same bag, he took the bag to the washroom. There he was "attacked by another man who I believed was making an attempt upon my life." Cranfill further stated that "[W]hen the attack upon me was made I grasped the pistol as if by instinct and in the scuffle that ensued it was twice discharged. I had no purpose of injuring my assailant and acted solely in self defense. When I found that he was powerless to hurt me, I did not harm him, though I had ample opportunity to do so."[33]

Since Cranfill was attempting to keep the incident as quiet as possible, Hayden depicted the event as he believed Cranfill was reporting it to the few individuals he told. Hayden told Cranfill's purported account in his *Complete Conspiracy* book. In this version, Hayden maintained that the night before Cranfill was to leave for the SBC, his son had asked him to take his pistol, since Hayden's son had recently knocked Cranfill down with his cane. Cranfill forbade his son to place the gun in his bag, but he did so anyway. Cranfill entered the washroom first and then Hayden entered a few minutes later as two other men exited. Cranfill then claimed that Hayden approached him from behind. Cranfill stated that he believed that Hayden had a weapon, so he pulled out his own pistol. Hayden then stated that he grabbed Cranfill, they wrestled to the floor, and two rounds were discharged. Hayden then claimed that Cranfill had bragged that he could have killed Hayden if he had so desired, but he (Cranfill) had the situation under control.

As one would expect, Hayden remembered the encounter somewhat differently. Unlike Cranfill, Hayden publicized every detail of the account in his *Complete Conspiracy.* He claimed that as he arose to enter the washroom, Reverend J. J. Kellam, pastor of First Baptist Oak Cliff, told him that Cranfill was just ahead of him. Hayden did not seem to care and continued toward the washroom. There were two other men and Cranfill in the washroom when Hayden entered.

The two other men left the washroom and Cranfill closed the gap between himself and his old rival. Hayden then claims that Cranfill said, "There is no one in here now but you and me, and if it were not for my self-respect, I would kill you. And if you ever print or mention my name again, I will kill you—." Hayden claimed that Cranfill swore at him over and over again, but Hayden ignored him. Evidently, Cranfill then walked behind Hayden and blocked the doorway. He then came even closer to Hayden with his language becoming fouler and more agitated. From the corner of his eye, Hayden saw the pistol in Cranfill's hand. Hayden grabbed for it. He remembered that J. H. Luther had told him that Cranfill had threatened "to take a shotgun, come to Dallas and blow his brains out." Cranfill tripped over a seat and they wrestled each other to the floor. During this scuffle, the pistol discharged twice into the ceiling. Hayden pinned Cranfill to the floor, placing his knee on Cranfill's chest while keeping both hands on the gun. The two continued to grapple for control of the weapon.

The conductor and other men burst into the washroom and managed to wrestle the gun away from Cranfill. The train soon stopped at Texarkana and Hayden went to find a policeman. However, upon Hayden's return to the train, Cranfill had fled. Cranfill was later found in the Huckins House on the Arkansas side of the city, was arrested, and released on a $1000 bond.[34] This event never went to civil or criminal trial. This in itself was amazing, since there had been so many lawsuits filed between the two men across the years.

Hayden believed that he had done nothing wrong and had merely acted in self-defense. Cranfill, however, was deeply disturbed by the incident. Whether it was his fault or not, it was his gun that was fired aboard the train. He believed that such a display was unbecoming for a minister and would bring unwanted censure to his church, the First Baptist Church of Dallas. Cranfill, therefore, on May 27, 1904, submitted his ministerial credentials to the First Church. In his accompanying report to the church, he claimed that he had acted in self-defense and that he was sorry for his actions. He asked for the church's forgiveness and that it not "forgive me half-heartedly and turn the cold shoulder to me as I shall be among you once again. I would rather be an alien than to just be tolerated." After receiving the letter, the church appointed a committee to investigate the incident as a matter of church discipline.

Following a two-month investigation, the committee, led by deacon W. L. Williams, came to the conclusion that Cranfill had not acted wrongfully and the church returned his ministerial credentials. One might expect this verdict in Cranfill's favor, for the First Baptist Church of Dallas loved Cranfill. In addition, his exoneration was tatamount to a guilty verdict for Hayden. It seems ironic that since many of the episodes which dominated the previous twenty years of Texas Baptist life grew from the original conflicts at the First Baptist Church of Dallas, the last scene also occurred in one of its then-famous committee investigations. Despite his exoneration by the church committee, Cranfill was crushed by the ordeal. In the May 26, 1904, edition of the *Baptist Standard*, Cranfill resigned as editor and sold the newspaper to J. H. Gambrell.

In 1905 Hayden's litigation against several leaders of the BGCT came to a close. Two of the trials ended in a hung jury, although Hayden claimed the reason he did not receive an outright victory with one of the hung juries was due to the fact that Cranfill's lawyer, H. E. Cullom, bribed the jury.[35] This accusation may actually have been true as Cullom and defendant C. C. Slaughter's lawyer, G. G. Wright, were both arrested for bribery, fined, and eventually jailed.

The other two trials, however, were outright victories for Hayden. Appeals were filed on both sides. The trials finally ended when Cranfill, without informing his fellow defendants, settled the suits.[36] Three cases were on the docket when Cranfill brought the trials to a conclusion. He paid $100 to settle each suit. The overall cost to Cranfill, however, was much greater than $300. When all the litigation, lawyer's fees, and court costs were accumulated, Cranfill claims to have spent more than $25,000 out of his own pocket in defense of the Convention.[37] By doing so, he hoped to remove Hayden from the limelight and to stop the rancor that had become identified with the Convention.[38] The good name of several Texas Baptists had been soiled and the reputation of the Convention had been severely damaged.[39] With this action, the Hayden Controversy came to a close. Hayden, however, had already lost much of his denominational sway years earlier by means of the several adroit actions taken by the BGCT.

CHAPTER 8

YESTERDAY AND TODAY

THE FINAL DECADES OF the nineteenth century were periods of transformation and controversy for Texas Baptists. The denomination's forefathers who established the Baptist presence in Texas were slowly passing from the scene. This change in leadership was embodied in the rising influence of B. H. Carroll, J. M. Carroll, R. C. Buckner, J. B. Gambrell, and J. B. Cranfill. These five men personified the vision of the new BGCT, and their presence dominated Texas Baptist life for several decades. Moreover, Samuel Augustus Hayden was also a leader in Texas Baptist life who took a significant leadership role in the BGCT's years of transformation. Hayden's inability to garner the support necessary to change the course of denominational life led to the continuation and escalation of a controversy that was already in motion. Although Hayden eventually failed, this study supports several new conclusions regarding him and his role in Texas Baptist life between 1877 and 1901.

The Hayden Controversy began well before Hayden arrived in Dallas, for its roots are to be found in the Waco Policy. Anchored by B. H. Carroll and the BGA, the Waco Policy desired that the locus of all denominational, administration, and educational institutions be centered in Waco. In 1875, R. C. Buckner was employed as the editor of the *Texas Baptist* in order to advance this cause and garner support for Waco University. J. B. Link, editor of the *Texas Baptist Herald*, was a BSC advocate and supporter of Baylor University at Independence. He too was for the centralization of the Baptist schools, but did not advocate Waco as the place for such centralization. He believed a more neutral site was needed. These men were both members of the First Baptist Church of Dallas, were champions of their different perspectives, and used their newspapers to advance their causes.

Because Pastor Curry of the First Baptist Church of Dallas spoke out against the Waco Policy at the 1879 BGA, his church was drawn into the Controversy. In order to help fight the Waco Policy and secure some future status for Dallas, J. B. Link was permitted to join the First Baptist Church of Dallas under usual circumstances. This split the church, promoted acrid newspaper allegations, and led to a one-sided trial before the BGA in 1880 over which congregation was the true First Baptist Church of Dallas. It was after these events that Hayden came to Dallas and accepted the pastorate of the schismatic Live Oak Church in 1883.

Soon after his arrival in Dallas, Hayden bought Buckner's newspaper. After helping reconcile the two factions of the First Church of Dallas and create the BGCT, he secured Link's newspaper at the 1886 annual session of the BGCT. Hayden now had the only denominational organ in Texas. His problem, however, was that in order to secure the paper, he had to remain loyal to his Dallas following and ensure that the periodical would remain in their city. This mitigated against the Waco Policy, and especially against B. H. Carroll, who would have further prospered had the newspaper been located in Waco. These schismatic decisions placed these ambitious and influential men perpetually against each another. This conclusion is evidenced by the R. T. Hanks trial, the Dallas Missions meeting confrontation, the argument over Carroll's evening sermons, and Carroll's role in Hayden's removal from the BGCT, pointing to an undue amount of attention placed on the Hayden-Cranfill imbroglio.

Just as Hayden and B. H. Carroll were rivals, so also were the cities of Dallas and Waco. This rivalry was already in place, but it grew stronger under the negative interaction between Hayden and Carroll. The examples of this aspect of the Hayden Controversy are glaring: Pastor Curry's first volley against the Waco Policy; B. H. Carroll's meddling in the BGA trial of the First Church of Dallas to secure a Buckner faction victory in 1883; Hayden's election and maintenance of a newspaper presence in Dallas rather than in Waco; the birth of the *Baptist Standard*; and the change of the venue for the 1897 BGCT. This rivalry may also be noted in Hayden's realization that he had little chance of regaining his seat at the 1898 Waco Convention, but his belief that his chances for being seated were excellent at the Dallas Convention of 1899. Hayden and Carroll were the respective champions of Dallas and Waco. Hence, these cities were rivals within the Convention, but not for ecclesiological reasons. The rivalry seemed more to do with civic pride and the maintenance of a constituency than any other reason.

Furthermore, even though R. T. Hanks' role in the birth of the *Baptist Standard* is undisputed, more than likely a newspaper in Waco would have developed regardless of his personal controversy with Hayden. Unlike Buckner, who printed a tremendous amount of material concerning Waco, Hayden did not ignore the city, but neither did he cater to Waco's wish to be copiously represented. R. T. Hanks' willingness to start a paper may have been little more than an excuse to develop a denominational organ that would be located in and represent the interests of Waco.

Even though Hayden's reform movement may have had valid points, it also seemed to have been fueled by the personal spite he felt for the Carroll brothers. In particular, Hayden's dispute with the Carrolls intensified after the debate over B. H. Carroll's sermons. Whether he wanted to publish the sermons or not, to have them removed from his newspaper in full view of the whole state was an embarrassing situation for Hayden. Despite the facts that Cranfill lost his financial records and his newspaper office mysteriously burned to the ground, the presence of nepotism on the Board, and J. M. Carroll's apparently high salary as Corresponding Secretary, Hayden's continued accusations against these men after their exonerations point not only to his desire for reform, but also his attempt to invoke vengeance upon those whom he perceived to be intent on debilitating his editorial influence within the denomination. From this point forward, all editorial caution on both sides of the controversy was absent, and a full-fledged newspaper war ensued.

Additionally, the Hayden Controversy should not be perceived as an Americanized version of the Gospel Missions Movement. T. P. Crawford, the author of the Gospel Missions Movement, believed that "missionaries should be sent out only by local churches, not by mission boards. This, he believed, was the *gospel* method, hence the name of the movement. He felt that for a mission board to appoint, set salaries, and give directions for missionaries was tantamount to an episcopal function."[1] At no point did Hayden advance this mode of operation. Hayden was a member of the Board of the BGCT as late as 1894. When Hayden spoke out against the Board, he was speaking out against certain members of the Board who, he perceived, were dominating virtually all of the BGCT's affairs and possibly covering up their roles in some unusual activities. Uncovering and disseminating these activities, as well as correcting them, were the goals of the Reform Movement. The accusations against Hayden that implied he was a Crawfordist were rooted in articles in the *Missionary Worker* and the *Baptist Standard* that either insinuated or clearly stated that he supported this movement. The publication of these accusations appears to have been a conscious strategy of the anti-Haydenite faction in order to sway the allegiance of some of Hayden's followers to back the BGCT Board. Hayden flatly denied the allegations in several editions of the *Texas Baptist and Herald*. He did not, however, help his own cause by maintaining that the Board was an episcopacy and J. B. Gambrell was the "pontiff."

It should also be noted that Hayden, even though he was not a Crawfordist, was a Landmarkist. His argument for the sovereign church's right to seat its own duly elected messengers and his denial of the Convention's right to remove them were Landmarkist tenets. However, B. H. Carroll, J. M. Carroll, J. B. Cranfill, and J. B. Gambrell were also Landmarkists.[2] For whatever reason, this latter group appears to have been more selective in the Landmarkist tenets it upheld. Being an advocate of Landmarkism in Texas was not considered atypical and it must be remembered that the Hayden Controversy began years before the sovereign church versus the Board argument had ever come into play. The controversy was never about ecclesiology. When the Hayden Controversy is examined in its totality, other reasons appear more logical: primarily, Hayden's desire for recognition in the Convention, the Waco Policy, a power struggle with B. H. Carroll, Hayden's belief that the *Baptist Standard* was trying to stifle his voice in denominational affairs, and his incessant and often baseless attacks on the Board. Ecclesiology was present at the very end, but it was always a secondary aspect of the Hayden Controversy. The leaders of the BGCT must have believed that as long as Hayden and his followers could be seated and continually disrupt their proceedings, the Baptist denomination's growth in Texas would be retarded and never fully prosper. For this reason, Hayden's adversaries may have been willing to redefine some of their own ecclesiological beliefs in order to remove Hayden from their midst.

Despite the venom spewed by the combatants, the Hayden Controversy significantly strengthened the Baptist General Convention of Texas on at least two fronts. It helped remove those individuals who were against the organized work as authorized by the current members of the Executive Board. There seemed to be no possible way that Hayden's faction and the BGCT could ever work together, given the personalities involved. Whether it was over an ecclesiological technicality or a distrust of the Board, the birth of the BMA strengthened the BGCT. When the BMA was formed, a peace fell upon the BGCT that allowed the work to move forward in a more stable manner. Though initially it appeared as if the BGCT was hemorrhaging members, by 1905 many of the less troublesome churches that joined the BMA came to realize that the new organization would not work, and they returned to the BGCT. In this case, the denominational schism served to force the two groups to define and clarify their positions and thus led to a more positive outcome.

The Hayden Controversy also demonstrated that the BGCT was strong enough to withstand a major controversy. The survival of the Convention was due to the new leadership. Though the action of some of the leaders on both sides appears at times less than ethical, these individuals helped preserve the Baptist cause in Texas. The men who took the lead during this critical time of transition and controversy were the same individuals who built not only a viable structure for the propagation of the gospel in Texas, but also the formation of Southwestern Baptist Theological Seminary. Therefore, the treacherous events during this period brought to light the strengths of several men who would dedicate the remainder of their lives to the service of the Baptist General Convention of Texas and the Southern Baptist Convention.

The current struggle between the Baptist General Convention of Texas and the Southern Baptists of Texas has several similarities to the Hayden Controversy. Like the participants in the Hayden Controversy, the two current factions, the BGCT and SBT, differ significantly over the role of the Executive Board, the messenger system, theological matters, and the dispersal of funds.[3] Although there are no dynamic leaders whom people would blindly follow involved in the current dispute, such as S. A. Hayden, J. B. Gambrell, and B. H. Carroll, there are strong-willed leaders bent on the defense of their organizations and their positions.

A major reason the BMA left the BGCT was its perception that the Executive Board of the BGCT dominated statewide Baptist polity. The BMA believed that there was too much bureaucracy in the BGCT, nepotism, and alienation of those whose theology differed from those currently in leadership positions. Hayden often described the Executive Board as a closed society that only accepted new members upon the basis of their support of the current Board. When Hayden's advocates like Rufus Burleson were removed from positions of influence, his Reform Movement was not taken seriously, and he was removed from the BGCT in 1897, he felt as if he had no other choice than to join the dissidents who were in the process of forming the Baptist Missionary Association.

The SBT has given a similar argument for its departure. Its leaders believe they have been locked out of the Executive Board and passed over for key positions because they have theological disagreements with the current BGCT leadership. Because they have been largely ignored for leadership positions and thus have been denied the opportunity to promote reforms within the BGCT, they argue that they had no other choice but to leave and form their own organization.

As was the situation during the Hayden Controversy, newspapers serve as the voice of the BGCT and SBT. The papers support the positions taken by each of the organizations. The *Baptist Standard* was created in 1888 by several members of the BGCT to combat Hayden's accusations in the *Texas Baptist Herald*. The leaders of the BGCT accused Hayden of unbalanced representation of the controversial issues of the day, and they felt as if they had no choice but to start a paper to present their side of the issues. This led to the newspaper war that dominated the last decade of the nineteenth century.

The future SBT members also believed that their side of the contested issues were either being misrepresented or ignored by those who publish the *Baptist Standard*.[4] In order to present their points of view to Texas Baptists, they also believed they had no other choice than to create the independently published *Plumbline* in 1997. Before the SBT became a fully operating and incorporated body, the *Plumbline* served as the organization's unofficial voice. With the official birth of the SBT in November of 1998, the *Plumbline* ceased publication and the *Southern Baptist Texan* became its official periodical.

The current relationship between the *Southern Baptist Texan* and the *Baptist Standard* is as strained as was the relationship between the *Baptist Standard* and the *Texas Baptist Herald* in the nineteenth century. During the Hayden Controversy, either newspaper was equally as likely to cast a stone at the other with little or no provocation. The current SBT/BGCT newspaper conflict is more defensive than offensive. In virtually each issue of their respective newspapers each group examines the other's policies and points out their differences. In this respect, the current conflict does qualify as a newspaper controversy, but not at the same level as the Hayden Controversy.

The Executive Committee's use of money was a primary issue during the Hayden Controversy. The Hayden faction believed that the Corresponding Secretary was overpaid, fiscal aid was given primarily to the urban churches to the detriment of the country churches, and that churches should not be able to buy extra seats at the annual Convention. During the Reform Movement, Hayden pressed these problematic issues, but found no satisfaction. When the constitution of the BMA was ratified, these problematic issues were eliminated.

The group that later became the SBT complained against the redirection of money as recommended in the BGCT's Effectiveness/Efficiency Committee (E/EC) report, which was ratified in 1997. The group also had differences of opinion with issues such as the BGCT's position on more local church work in Texas rather than through the North American Mission Board of the SBC; the ability to work with other evangelistic organizations, such as the Cooperative Baptist Fellowship; the financial support of independent Texas theological schools rather than only the Southern Baptist Convention seminaries; and a voluntary lay foreign mission program separate from the Southern Baptist Convention's International Mission Board. The SBT claimed that these referendums were meant to sever the BGCT's ties with the SBC and, in essence, make the BGCT a national convention. The SBT leadership believed that this change forced people to choose whether they wanted to be Texas Baptists or Southern Baptists.[5] The SBT chose to be Southern Baptists.

As in the Hayden Controversy, the convention messenger system was at the heart of the matter. As defined in the BGCT constitution of 1886, a contributing church could send two messengers and an additional messenger for each $25 contributed. No church could register more than eight messengers. Because Hayden's power base was always in the rural, less financially stable churches, he complained that by being able to buy additional seats, the larger, more financially stable churches could dominate the Convention. He blamed the messenger system for his removal from the BGCT Convention in 1897. Though the cost and number of messengers permitted increased over the years, the same messenger system remained in place until the ratification of the EE/C report in 1997.

The SBT believed that the new messenger system was meant to ensure the inability of their advocates to advance their reforms in Convention matters. The old system now allowed for each church to send four messengers for its first one hundred members. Another messenger could also be sent for each additional one hundred members with a maximum of twenty-five messengers. The new system adopted in the

E/EC referendum allowed two messengers for the first one hundred members and a $250 gift to the BGCT merited two additional representatives. For an additional $1,000 a church could send one representative per hundred members of the congregation. This allowed smaller churches to send at least two representatives to the annual Convention, and for a small fee it could send four. If the SBT advocates did not want their money to go to BGCT functions, they would have only nominal representation. This also balanced out the power between the smaller churches and the SBT mega-churches. The smaller churches outnumbered the mega-churches to such a degree that the mega-churches could no longer pack the Convention with their representatives. Though disliked by the SBT, this new messenger system is almost identical to the system used by the Southern Baptist Convention. As in the Hayden Controversy, the direction of funds and the messenger system were volatile issues. The modern controversy and Hayden Controversy are also similar in the manner that the argument, though it is actually over power, has taken on the auspice of ecclesiology.

Unlike the Hayden Controversy, however, the ramifications of this controversy extend well beyond the scope of Texas. Because the SBT stated "that they are the arm of the Southern Baptist Convention in Texas,"[6] they have defined themselves in national terms rather than in state terms. For all intents and purposes, they are the Southern Baptist Convention's satellite organization in Texas and thus a lower level of an episcopal structure. Unlike the Hayden Controversy, which resulted in the birth of a new state organization (BMA), the current struggle has resulted in the birth of a new branch of the Southern Baptist Convention (SBT).

Another significant difference may be found in the organic relationship between the two groups after the schismatic faction formed its own organization. When the BMA advocates left the BGCT in 1900, they completely left. They were so disgusted with the BGCT that they wanted nothing to do with it. Though they cast an occasional stone at the BGCT in the *Texas Baptist Herald*, they did not go to the BGCT annual Convention, those with positions in the BGCT resigned, and there were no dually aligned churches.

In the current situation, all of the advocates of the SBT have not left the BGCT. In fact, the SBT has encouraged churches to maintain some of their ties to the BGCT. Some of these churches still give money to BGCT and thus are eligible to send messengers to the annual session of the BGCT.

While the future of the current differences between the SBT and the BGCT is unclear, it is doubtful that the future of the controversy will resemble the outcome of the Hayden Controversy. During the Hayden Controversy, the BMA had little money, few workers, and never developed into a major convention. After some initial excitement over the new convention, the majority of the BMA churches returned to the BGCT. As of 1995, the BMA had only 498 churches in Texas. The BGCT not only survived the schism, but had grown to 4,658 churches by 1995.

On the other hand, the SBT is well financed and is backed by the Southern Baptist Convention. The BGCT has been able to cope without the SBT's members, but not without its money. This fiscal problem has led to the elimination of jobs from the BGCT staff, and by all appearances, it appears that more will occur. The SBT is growing, as did the BMA in its earliest days, and it continues to grow. The SBT, however, still does not have nearly the number of churches as does the BGCT. Given the fact that the BGCT is so well established it is difficult to see the SBT approach its numbers in the foreseeable future. Because of the SBT's desire to form a strong relationship with the Southern Baptist Convention and the BGCT's desire for a less controlling national body, however, it does appears that the consequences of the current controversy will affect Baptist life in Texas to a far greater extent than did the Hayden Controversy.

APPENDIX A

Dallas Church Vindicated

Official Statement
Of Facts by the First Baptist Church at Dallas, Texas

The First Baptist Church at Dallas, Texas, met January 7, 1880, pursuant to adjournment, there being about one hundred and fifty members present. After worship and some preliminary business, the following paper was read and unanimously adopted, as an official expression of the church, to-wit:

Whereas, at the last regular conference of the First Baptist Church, of Dallas, Texas, held December 24, 1879, a part of our membership, embracing about one-fifth of the church, at the instance, and on behalf of Elder R. C. Buckner, as we believe, presented to this church a "Memorial," in which they make grave charges and reflections against the church, placing us in a false light before the denomination.

Now, therefore, in the interest of truth and justice, and in vindication of the church, in view of these aspersions, we, the First Baptist Church, of Dallas, Texas, in conference assembled, hereby declare and make known the following

STATEMENT OF FACTS.

At our regular conference, November 18, 1879, Brother W.N. Griffeth offered the following resolution, to-wit:

WHEREAS, Brothers J.B. Link and R.C. Buckner do not entertain for each other such feelings as become Christian brethren, and as brethren have labored with them privately and tried to effect a reconciliation, and have failed in every instance, and, as the breach between these brethren is growing wider every day, and is working to the detriment of the First Baptist Church, of Dallas, and as there is no indication that the breach will be closed by any act of themselves: Be it therefore

Resolved, That the First Baptist Church of Dallas, Texas, appoint her deacons and six other brethren—three of the latter to be chosen by Brother R.C. Buckner and three by Brother J.B. Link, and six brethren to select a seventh and they and the Deacons to investigate at once the differences existing between Brother J.B. Link and R.C. Buckner; and if possible settle the same, and if they fail to do so, report to the church the result of their investigations and labors, together with all the evidence taken, and the church then deal with said brethren as she thinks best, but nothing in this resolution contained, binding the church to decide between said brethren, upon the evidence collated by said committee, but the evidence may be reheard by the church.

This resolution was adopted and Brother Griffeth was appointed a committee of one to notify Elders Link and Buckner of its contents, and report to the clerk of the church the names of those they might appoint. At our regular conference meeting, December 24th, 1879, he reported as follows:

To the First Baptist Church: "Having been appointed by the church at our last conference a committee of one to notify Elders R. C. Buckner and J. B. Link, of the action of the church in ordering a committee to be raised to adjust, if possible, the matter of difference between these brethren, also to receive the names of the committeemen to be selected by them, I ask leave to submit the following report. As soon as practicable I notified these brethren of the action of the church in the premises, and requested them to furnish me the names of the committeemen each were required by the church to choose, to complete the committee, whereupon Brother J.B. Link furnished the names of his part of the committee, but in consequence of Brother R.C. Buckner's having failed and refused to select the number required of him to complete the committee, the same has never been organized, and no steps have been taken to effect the settlement between these two brethren, as contemplated by the church, wherefore I ask to be relieved from further duty in this behalf.

W.N. GRIFFETH

Brother Griffeth went to elder Buckner several times during the month to know if he had appointed his part of the committee. A few days prior to the conference of December 24th, he notified Brother Griffeth that he would not appoint, and would give his reasons to the church. His friends having suggested that there was objections to the deacons acting on his committee, Brother Griffeth had the following resolution ready in writing to propose at the conference of the 24th supposing it would be satisfactory to all parties, to-wit:

WHEREAS, The committee sought to be raised by a former resolution of the church, passed at one last conference, for the purpose of effecting a friendly settlement of the personal differences between our brethren R. C. Buckner and J. B. Link, have taken no steps to bring about a reconciliation from the fact that the committee has not been completed, Brother Buckner having failed to appoint his part of the committee as required by the resolution, and

WHEREAS, Objections have been made to the committee and the manner of appointing the same.

Therefore be it

Resolved, That the committee heretofore appointed be discharged, and that Brothers R. C. Buckner and J. B. Link be, and they are hereby required by the First Baptist Church, of Dallas, Texas, to appoint, by next Wednesday night, each five discreet brethren, members of this church, and the ten thus appointed to select one other, making a committee of eleven, whose sole duty it shall be, in the spirit of brotherly love, to bring about a reconciliation of the differences between these brethren, in accordance with the rules prescribed by our Saviour, in the 18th Chapter of Matthew.

W.N. GRIFFETH

But before Brother Griffeth could get an opportunity to offer this last resolution, and immediately on the reading of his report as a committee of one, and on its adoption, Elder Buckner arose and requested the privilege of giving his reasons for not appointing his part of the committee, which was granted. He proceeded to read a paper in which he was understood to decline amenability to this church. On closing that document, he drew another from his pocket, and proceeded to read a paper styled, "A memorial addressed to the First Baptist Church, at Dallas, Texas," making grave charges against the church, gotten up, as we believe, by Elder Buckner and a few of his sympathizers, to shield him from an apprehended exposure of his conduct toward Elder Link, if the matter was allowed to progress. The steps so far taken by the church, however, only looked to an amicable settlement of differences between these brethren. This was an end most earnestly desired, not only by us, but probably by the denomination at large. We were apprised that Elder Buckner claimed to have grievances against Elder Link. We had patiently and long waited for him to take scriptural steps to settle them. The church has acted throughout all these matters, with the greatest forbearance, and its whole course has been conciliatory. While it could not be governed by the dictates of any one man, or even of several, it has maintained a disposition to conciliate, and the wishes of the majority have sometimes been held in abeyance out of respect to a few. It has assiduously guarded against irritation and has been constantly disposed to heal every alienation. While we have been waiting and thus forbearing, Elder Buckner has failed to take any steps toward conciliation, but has in various ways apparently sought to undermine the pastor, injure the church and its interests, and with a few under his immediate control, sought, and did poison the minds of as many of the membership as possible. It was thought also that if the matter could be settled, where he pretend to have a special grievance, the rest would be easily adjusted.

But two courses were open to the church; one was to demand of Elder Buckner to take scriptural steps for a reconciliation with Elder Link, Elder Buckner being the aggrieved party—Elder Link having made no complaints of lack of fellowship. The other was to appoint a fair and discreet committee to see these brethren, talk with them, investigate and understand the difficulty as far as need be, and settle it if possible. This seemed the milder way of reaching it, and most likely to succeed, and was adopted. Brother Griffeth, who was on intimate terms, and in special sympathy, with Elder Buckner, both personally and in general plans of work, and at the time doing special work on his paper, on his own motion, and on his own responsibility, got up the resolution and presented it to the church. Elder Link objected to Brother Griffeth that the preamble placed him in an unfair light, but Brother Griffeth said he must place both on an equality, and Elder Link acquiesced.

We believe that Brother Griffeth acted with the conviction that the matter could and would be settled. No one probably supposed that Elder Buckner would or could refuse, or would avoid an effort to settle the difficulty or shrink from the fullest investigation, if it should come to that, after having said so much and claimed to have so many charges against Elder Link. If he did not like the course proposed by the church and suggested by the wisdom of his personal friend, it was his privilege to point out any other scriptural course towards a settlement. His positive refusal now forces the unwelcome conviction that since he came to Dallas, he has determined to rule this church; that he was even crystallizing a party around him before Elder Link came to Dallas, and sought through them to control the pastorate of the church and make it subservient to his own private interests; failing in this he sought to dictate to the church who might or might not join it, and failing in this and other efforts, he and a few sympathizers now seek to divide the church and to usurp its name, its rights and its prerogatives. These efforts culminated in the "Memorial" he read on the night of December 24th above referred to.

MEMORIAL REVIEWD.

This "Memorial," so-called, is a most extraordinary document to emanate from intelligent men and women professing Christianity. The signers, with three or four exceptions, as we understand it, had to depend on these three or four for most of their information, and some of them for all of it; and these three or four had to depend on Elder Buckner for a part of theirs.

First—It was presented at a time when nothing has been proposed by the church, but an effort to amicably settle known differences between two brethren, members of this church, and at a time when nothing was intended on the part of any member but a further effort in this same direction.

Second—It claims to be a memorial. A memorial is usually a representation of facts, accompanied with a petition to some legislative, or other body, to secure some action on the part of the body memorialized. But this document proposes no manner of adjusting admitted differences. It simply recites pretended grievances, and that "we," the fifty-nine signers, "must, and do, hold in disfellowship as church," the remaining two hundred and fifty, or more, members, and "maintain that we only, and all who coincide with us, are entitled to the name First Baptist Church, at Dallas, Texas." We hold, as members of a Baptist Church, that these brethren, if they were not satisfied with the efforts of the church to reconcile two of its members, should have proposed some better method to secure this end, instead of forestalling such efforts and joining on the parties in his denial of amenability to the church. We hold this conduct as at variance with all Baptist Church usage, and so far as we know, without a single precedent in our denominational and church history.

Third—As to the statements recited as facts, we submit that they are mostly not facts, and we instance the following, leaving other things unnoticed for the sake brevity:

FIRST STATEMENT.

The first statement of assumed facts in this "Memorial" is as follows: "It is a fact, well and generally known, that prior to Elder J. B. Link's application for membership in the Dallas Church, certain members of this church did not fellowship him because of certain allegations published in the Baptist Herald, and because of private statements made by him in conversation with brethren evidently designed to injure R.C. Buckner in business, and generally reflecting on his veracity and candor, and his sincerity as a Christian minister. It was known that this disfellowship was not at all confined to R.C. Buckner, and that other brethren avowed their purpose to vote against his reception if he should apply for membership."

Such a fact, so far from being "well and generally known" was not known to any one voting for Elder Link's reception, and is not believed now to be a fact. We believe that Elder Buckner made no objection. No other member of this church would ever have thought of making any, and that any other proposing to object only proposed to do so on his behalf. Brother Thomas A. Webb, who said much more, perhaps, than anybody else, and seemed really to be the only active man on Elder Buckner's behalf, said in this church on November 19th, 1879, publicly, that he had nothing personal against Brother Link. Brother W. H. Prather's objection referred to in another part of that document, was never heard of by those voting for Elder Link's reception, or that even he would object at all, till the question of rescinding came up. Brother Webb stated to the pastor that he and several others would object. The pastor pressed him for their names; he finally said that Brother Callaway would object. No other names were given or known to the pastor, or to Elder Link, or to those voting.

AN IMPORTANT FACT.

Elder Buckner had published his grievances and objections, and when he had utterly refused to lay these before a committee, half of his own choosing and all members of his own church, and to make them good, and had utterly refused to meet Elder Link fact to fact, on such a proposition, and try to settle the matters at issue, it was believed that no reasonable man could any longer object on Elder Buckner's behalf. Brother Callaway was present when Elder Link was received and did not object as Brother Webb said he would. The stated fact in this first paragraph is not a fact.

SECOND STATEMENT—IMPORTANT ANSWER.

It is stated that it "was not the time for a regular or stated conference," but "only a prayer meeting." If this were true the church was in the habit of receiving members at the Wednesday night prayer meetings, and it was therefore, an appropriate occasion for the reception of Elder J. B. Link or any one else. But that it was "only a prayer meeting" is not true. A conference had been called on the Sunday previous, for Monday night, on very important business relating to financial transactions with the trustees of Dallas College. The attendance on that night was not considered large enough and the conference adjourned to Wednesday night, and was regularly called to order and did transact its business. It was not only a prayer meeting but a conference meeting also.

THIRD STATEMENT.

It is stated that the pastor was urged on the evening of that day by an objector "not to give an opportunity for the reception of members on any occasion, unless a respectable number of members were present." The pastor has no recollection of any such urging, or even request, on that occasion. Two other brethren were with him during his interview with this supposed objector, and they have no recollection of it. One of them urged this brother to be at church and he did not decide whether he would come or not.

FOURTH STATEMENT—VERY IMPORTANT ANSWER.

The statement is made, that "it is in evidence that an unfinished correspondence looking to an adjustment of these differences, before application should be made for membership, was then pending."

This is not true. Elder Link and other members of this church were informed that Elder Buckner refused every proposition made to him for an adjustment. Until Elder Link had this information he did not propose to join the church.

IMPORTANT FACTS.

The facts are that no objection was even heard from Elder Buckner till Elder Link and his family had moved to the city of Dallas, bringing letters with them. Elder Link, himself, had been here sometime previously. Elder Buckner now told the pastor and others that he would object to Elder Link's holding membership with him in the same church. He was advised by a friend to file or deposit his objections with the pastor or clerk, and they would be on hand whether he was there or not. This he refused, or failed to do. He was visited by the pastor, and a sort of self-constituted committee of deacons, and his personal friends, who urged him to waive his objections, or try to settle all differences. This he refused. In a few weeks he published an article in the *Texas Baptist*, of May 23, 1878, under the head of "Called to Our Defense," which contained several allegations against Elder Link, of things published in the *Texas Baptist Herald*, and things reported to him as having been said, and devoting one part of the article to a very severe attack on Elder Link, in a matter no way concerning himself, and about which he needed no self-defense. This article was widely circulated among the membership of the church, and at the time created quite a prejudice, as was natural, against Elder Link and in favor of Elder Buckner. Elder Link seeing this article, the following correspondence ensued immediately:

IMPORTANT CORRESPONDENCE

DALLAS, Texas, May 24, 1878.

ELDER R.C. BUCKNER—Dear Brother—I see in the *Texas Baptist*, of this week, extensive reference to our personal relations, and I have heard, also, that you are disposed to object to my holding membership in the same church with you. I am surprised at some of the things you publish, and think there is a wide misapprehension of the facts. I would suggest that we have an interview—either one alone or in the presence of the brethren, we may mutually agree upon—and talk over matters with a view to a clear and perfect understanding.

I do not know what day next week I can be in Dallas, but can let you know when I come, and if you are willing to such a conference, you will please inform me through the kindness of Brother J.L. Williams, who bears to you this note.

Respectfully, J.B. Link

IMPORTANT MATTERS TO BE OBSERVED AND REMEMBERED.

Let it be observed, that Elder Buckner, claimed to be the aggrieved party, but refused or failed to seek a private conference with Elder Link, as the scriptures require, and that he might ascertain, whether his grievances were well or ill founded, but instead, published them to the world, to the injury of Elder Link, and circulated them extensively to poison and prejudice the membership of this church. Let it be observed and remembered that he has since diligently sought to make the impression that he refused to refer matters to a committee because there had been things published by Elder Link too bad to be referred to a conference at all, which he has claimed must be publicly withdrawn before a conference could be submitted to, while no such objection appears in his final letter to Elder Link, and was clearly an afterthought, to shield him from blame. And to have made such a demand would have been to *demand a concession of the very things in controversy*, and which only an arbitration, such as was proposed, could settle.

Let it also be remembered that Elder Link, though not complaining, did propose to Elder Buckner a private conference, which he refused, and when asked to go before brethren, half of his own choosing, and all of his own church, and Elder Link pledging himself to abide the adjustment they might suggest as proper and fair, Elder Link waited for his answer several days, as the dates show. He had learned through the pastor, verbally, that Elder Buckner wholly declined to accept his proposition, and proposed nothing else, and other members had learned the same. Upon this information, he joined the church at the very first opportunity that presented itself, which was Wednesday night, June the 5th. The next day he received Elder Buckner's last letter above, dated June the 4th, the day previous to his joining the church, showing that the information on which he acted was positively correct.

A CONCLUSION SUBMITTED.

We submit that correspondence, looking to adjustment, had been closed, so far as Elder Buckner was concerned, on the day previous to Elder Link's joining the church, as both the date of his letter and the information on which Elder Link acted, prove. We submit that he had done all that any man could be required to do, and took the only step left him to take properly, under the circumstances, and the church could do nothing but receive him, and if any one had objections, it was his duty to be present and enter them. Then the church could have investigated the objections, and decided on their validity. The members had seen Elder Buckner's complaints, and when he refused to bring them to the light and test of a fair investigation, it was naturally concluded that they were without any foundation in fact. His delay and refusal had been a matter of general remark and known to a great many, if not all who took any interest in the matter.

NO PRINCIPLE OR USAGE VIOLATED.

In this procedure, the church has violated no principle of Baptist usage, of Christianity or of the New Testament. If Elder Buckner knew reasons why Elder Link should not belong to this church, it was his privilege and bounden duty to bring charges against him, and make them good by proofs. Had he done this, the church would have gladly heard him, and acted promptly. But we are forced to the unpleasant conviction that he had no valid objection or charge to bring that would, in his own judgment, bear investigation or action, and that he has studiously and persistently avoided all steps looking to a settlement of his grievances with Elder Link.

FOURTH STATEMENT—ABOUT NUMBER PRESENT.

It is asserted that it was "at night, when darkness, mud and wet prevailed," and "only eleven members were present." If this were true, our church regulations allow that two or three gathered together, are the church at its regular appointments. (*See constitution, Art. 2.*) But it was not raining, and the best recollection of some present is that there were at least eighteen or twenty members present, and others say at least twenty-five or thirty, and among them were representative men of the church, who are generally present. No one thought there were too few present to transact important business, and no one of us counted the actual number present as no job was being put up. *Not a single member of the church, nor any one present, knew, before going to the church, that Elder Link would present his letter*, and no one suggested that there were too few there to receive him. That Elder Buckner was not there, was no surprise to anybody, unless he had been expected to come to be on guard, for his attendance was far from regular, either on good or bad nights.

STATEMENT FIFTH—IMPORTANT ANSWER.

It is stated that this application was not made at some other time because "the objectors were present, but was purposely deferred to such time as the objection could be evaded and the brethren objecting robbed of their inalienable rights." In the first place Elder Link never proposed to join the church after he heard of Elder Buckner's objection, till he saw he could secure no settlement with him, and when that was made clear and satisfactory to himself, and to other members, he proceeded to join at the very first opportunity presenting itself, without any one knowing beforehand that he intended to do so. He had been informed of but two men who would object, and both on Elder Buckner's behalf; one of these we know was present. But instead of objecting he voted for his reception and gave him the right hand of fellowship.

SIXTH STATEMENT—THE RESCINDING EFFORT.

It is stated that "at the first conference meeting actually held after the reception of Elder Link, a motion was made to rescind the act of his reception."

The last regular conference is stated to have adjourned "to the next regular meeting." Elder Link had gone to Palo Pinto county on business, to return by that time. In his absence, and when it was impossible for him to get word and be present, Elder Buckner and a few of his friends, who had worked up several signers to a petition to rescind him out of the church, insisted that a meeting must be called at once, to hear them. This was granted, although Elder Link could not be present.

FREE DISCUSSION—MOTION LOST—REASONS.

After a full and free discussion the motion to rescind was lost on the ground, mainly, that it was against well-established Baptist usage to rescind a man out of the church, and contrary to right and justice. If Elder Buckner had failed to put in his objections by a refusal to file them, and not being present at Elder Link's reception, it was held that the proper and only thing for him to do was to bring his charges and make them good by the proofs. The motion to rescind was lost, forty-four to twenty-three, by count, those voting in the affirmative being those whom Elder Buckner had induced to prejudge the case by signing his petition to rescind.

A PRINCIPLE STATED.

It is a clear principle belonging to our polity, that if a church performs an act objectionable to any member, in his absence, he may get some one voting in the affirmative to move a reconsideration at the next meeting of the church, but if no one so voting will do so, he can go no further, but must submit. If not willing to do this and remain in the church, he can ask for a letter and join elsewhere. Baptist churches are usually governed by majorities, and have for their guidance well known unwritten laws, customs and usages, to guide them in their deliberation, and certainly they are not governed by the dictates of one man.

SEVENTH—AN AFFIRMATION ANSWERED.

It is affirmed that at this meeting "the privilege was denied to Elder R. C. Buckner to state the grounds of his objection and to defend himself against statements made by brethren at the time, damaging to himself." This is not true. Elder Buckner spoke from written notes, at one time for more than an hour by the watch, and the only objection made was to his reading his letters to Elder Link without also reading Elder Link's letters to him, and also, that the matter was irrelevant, the question being upon the motion to rescind. He had the privilege of full and free speech throughout, the moderator, Brother G. B. Leachman, deciding that he was entitled to proceed.

EIGHTH—THAT CENSURE.

It is said the minority have been the subjects of censure from the pulpit, the pastor on one occasion saying that "he was pastor of only a part of the church and that fact was a thorn in his side." This is a very strange thing to be called "censure," and show labor, even if it were true, but the pastor denies having said this, and no one has been found outside of this faction who claims to have ever heard him say it. The pastor did say, upon one occasion, in alluding to an unmanly attack made against him and his church by the Mission Board of the General Association, in their circular letter, styled "Plano and Pittsburg," (several members of this church being members of this board), that there were a few who did not regard him as their pastor and this was a thorn in his flesh.

NINTH—THAT COMMITTEE.

Referring to the committee to be appointed under Brother Griffeth's resolution, it is stated that "this committee was empowered to take evidence and report to the church, and therefore made the judge of such evidence as they would submit." If this were true, the resolution (see first resolution) distinctly states that the church shall not be bound by anything done by this committee. The committee had only power to try and settle the difficulty and report the result of their investigations and labors, with the evidence taken, to the church. That this committee had no power to try either of these parties is shown by the resolution itself, and it was so conceded and understood in the discussion upon its passage. Elder Buckner had the privilege of appointing three members on that committee, who had the right if they choose, to make a minority report. There could have been no trial of any one, because there was no one charged with any offense.

TENTH—AS TO PARTISANS.

It was also objected that "all resident deacons but one were strong and zealous partisans of J.B. Link, and pre-committed in this matter against R.C. Buckner." This the deacons disclaim, but say that whatever their opinions of the two brethren may be, that opinion is formed from their knowledge of the acts of these brethren, respectively. They disclaim any and all prejudice in favor of Elder Link, or against Elder Buckner, and say they greatly desired a reconciliation between them, and to that end could and would have faithfully and candidly investigated all matters of difference between the brethren, had the matter gone forward. That this objection was not well taken, the subsequent action, or rather inaction of the deacons proves. If a church cannot trust her tried officers to do right, whom can she trust? Elder Buckner himself, did not make this objection till he also repudiated the authority of the church. Had he objected, not one of them would have served on the committee. One of the deacons, for himself, so informed Brother Beddo, who was in Elder Buckner's employ. The complaint has been made that Elder Buckner was absent when this committee was raised. There was no need that he should have been present. Elder Link, also, at the suggestion of brethren, absented himself.

ELEVENTH—STATEMENT.

It is stated that "two of the deacons by motion and argument urged the appointment of themselves and their brother deacons." This is not true. But one deacon spoke upon the subject of their appointment, and he only in answer to unjust allusions made to the deacons. In speaking he constantly excepted himself and spoke of the rest as being above the littleness that had been attributed to them. He did not urge their appointment on the committee but only favored the raising of the committee to attend to the business.

TWELFTH AND FINAL.

Again it was said that "it was known that he (Brother Buckner), would not submit." No one knew or could have anticipated so extraordinary a procedure as that he would not submit to his own church in an effort to settle a difficulty between himself and a brother, with whom he was at variance.

Now, we have answered all the statements of the memorial we deem it worth while to notice. We champion the cause of no man but contend only for the right, for truth and justice according to the Scriptures and the best lights before us. We have simply sought to follow the path of duty in all this procedure.

APPENDIX B

The Memorial

A MEMORIAL ADDRESS TO THE FIRST BAPTIST CHURCH AT DALLAS, TEXAS.

Dear Brethren and Sisters:

Prompted by love to this church in particular, and to Baptist principles generally, we are painfully constrained to take the solemn step indicated in this memorial. Certain events developed in the last eighteen months of our church history make our duty plain, and, in our judgment, imperatively demand this course of action.

We desire, however, most respectfully, affectionately and sincerely to make one more appeal to you to pause and reflect upon your course in matters that have filled many hearts with sadness, disturbed the peace of the church, and resulted in great injury to the cause of Christ.

We desire first to recite certain generally received Baptist principles that from time immemorial have been cherished by our people. The Scriptures clearly compare the Church in its unity with a body and its members. They also declare that two cannot walk together unless they be agreed. They further show that a house divided against itself cannot stand. And moreover God's promises to bless His people conditioned upon their love and fellowship for each other. The prosperity, usefulness, and even the very existence of a church are made dependent on its unity.

For these reasons Baptist churches have always required unanimity in the reception of members, regarding it as suicidal to a church and treasonable to Christ knowingly to take a case of a discipline into its own bosom from without.

Now, we desire to show that in the reception of Elder J.B. Link, on Wednesday night, June 5th, 1878, and in subsequent events related thereto, these great principles of our common faith have been systematically violated.

(1) It is a fact well and generally known that prior to Elder Link's application for membership in Dallas church, certain members of this church did not fellowship him because of certain allegations published in the Baptist Herald, and because of private statements made by him in conversation with brethren evidently designed to injure Elder R. C. Buckner in business, and gravely reflecting on his veracity and candor and his sincerity as a Christian minister. It was known that this disfellowship was not at all confined to R.C. Buckner, and that other brethren had avowed their purpose to vote against his reception, if he should apply for membership. Now, we claim that Elder Link himself, the pastor of the church, and the deacon who made the motion for his reception, were each and all fully apprised and notified of the opposition to Elder Link's reception and the ground of it.

(2) It is a well known fact that the night Elder J.B. Link was received into the church was not a conference meeting, but a prayer meeting.

(3) It is in evidence that on an occasion appropriate for the reception of members, Elder Link and the objectors both being present, to the surprise of the objectors no opportunity for uniting with the church was given.

(4) It is in evidence that the assistant pastor did, on the day following Elder Link's reception, say as follows: "I expected him to join

last night, because it was a bad night and I did not think Brother Buckner would be there."

(5) It is in evidence that late in the evening of the day on which Elder Link was received at night, the pastor was notified by still another objector that, on account of serious illness in his family (his wife being then on her deathbed), he could not be out that night, and the objector, with special reference to his case, further urged the pastor not to give an opportunity for reception of members on any occasion, unless a respectable number of members were present.

(6) It is in evidence that an unfinished correspondence, looking to an adjustment of these difficulties before application should be made for membership, was then pending. This was known to the pastor, and on Tuesday (the day previous) the correspondent objecting notified him that he had a letter which he desired him, as his pastor, to inspect before its delivery to Elder Link, and not having time that evening, the pastor left an appointment for consultation on the letter the next day, but failed to fulfill it.

(7) It is also in evidence that yet another objector, absent the night of J.B. Link's reception, states that he heard him say that he did not think he could remain in Dallas that week beyond Monday night, upon which statement said objector supposed him out of the city on the night of his reception.

(8) Now, let it be added to all this that on the Tuesday night preceding the reception there was such a rainfall as, according to the Dallas Daily Herald, had not been witnessed in twenty years, and that on the very Wednesday in question the same paper further says: "Long after daybreak, and after the rain had ceased, the waters continued to rush with unabated fury through the main sewers, in many places carrying away the crossings over the gutters and doing other damage. Fences and other objects were swept away by the torrent that passed through them." Now, it was at night of this day, and on a night itself when darkness, mud and rain prevailed, that Elder Link's reception occurred. Only eleven members were present. Only eight of the eleven voted at all on his reception.

(9) From a consideration of all these points, and others not necessary to mention, we have been irresistibly driven to the mortifying conviction that this application was not only made on appropriate occasions because the objectors were present, but was purposely deferred to such time and under such circumstances as that the objections could be evaded and the brethren objecting robbed of their inalienable right to vote on the reception of applicants for membership, and state their objections, if any.

(10) This reception was known, the objectors determined to make a solemn appeal to the church in regular conference in the interest of justice and principle. At the time of the very next conference after the reception they were prepared to make an appeal, but a sermon was delivered, and afterwards, at the suggestion of the pastor as to the lateness of the hour, upon motion the Conference adjourned immediately to the next regular meeting. The motion, however, was discussed, but very important business demanded immediate attention.

(11) At the first Conference actually held after the reception of Elder Link a motion was made to rescind the act of his reception, on such grounds as have been recited, but a majority vote ratified the action of the eight members, whereupon twenty members of the church, all adults and heads of families, entered their solemn protest against the illegality of the proceedings and had their names entered on the minutes as then protesting.

(12) At the same time the privilege was denied to Elder R.C. Buckner to state the grounds of his objection and to defend himself against statements made by brethren at the time damaging to himself, although the Moderator had ruled in his favor. But candor demands the statement that Brother W.H. Prather was not prevented from making the plain declaration that he objected personally to J.B. Link's reception, on account of what he had long since said to him and of developments following thereafter.

(13) But matters have not stopped here. The then minority were not only deprived of their inalienable privileges as Baptist, but have been the subjects of censure from the pulpit, the pastor on one

occasion saying that he was pastor of only a part of the church, and that fact was a thorn in his side.

(14) For many long months the minority, as it then was, have suffered on, until finally it appears they are now denied even the poor privilege of patient sufferance.

(15) At the last Conference, and in the absence of R.C. Buckner, a motion was made to refer the adjustment of difficulties between him personally and J.B. Link to a committee consisting of the deacons of the church, and seven others, three each to be chosen by these two brethren, and another to be chosen by the six. This committee was empowered to take evidence and report to the Church, and therefore made the judge of such evidence as they would submit. A motion to provide for an investigation before the Church, instead of one before a committee, was lost. It was also objected that all the resident deacons but one were strong and zealous partisans of J. B. Link, and precommitted in this matter against R. C. Buckner; but this objection was also overruled by the dominant party, two of the deacons by motion and argument, urging the appointment of themselves and their brother deacons.

One of our brethren was thus not only denied the right of having his case investigated before the church, but was ordered to submit it, involving his character as a man, a Christian and minister, to the decision of a tribunal not only unscriptural is itself, and to which it was known he would not submit, but withal stocked against him, preventing the possibility of impartial proceedings.

(16) One object of this memorial is to hereby notify the Church that in all this matter we, the undersigned, each and all, make common cause, that we do not regard it as a case of personal grievance between two brethren simply, but as involving fundamental principles of Bible law. The unanimity of the Church on reception of members, the privileges of members, the impropriety of referring matters to committees that should, if at all, be investigated before the Church; the impropriety of trying cases where offenses were committed and known before church connections, and some other things, are all involved. And we do hereby notify

the Church that we all, whose names are hereunto appended, hold Elder J. B. Link in disfellowship, not being willing to regard him as a lawful member of this body, and that we respectfully, but emphatically, deny the right of the dominant party in this church to try any one or all of us for disfellowshipping him.

And we do now memorialize the members of this Church that we hold as anti-Baptistic and unscriptural all the proceedings held in this case, beginning with and including the reception of Elder J. B. Link, and so we will ever maintain; and that it is our fixed purpose to claim our rights, one and all of them, before this body, the denomination and the world; that we will make our appeal to the candid judgment of mankind on the simple facts in this case; and we know that some, and believe that many others, whose names are not appended to this paper, entertain the same views which we hold.

(17) And, finally, in kindness, sadness and love, we hereby announce to the heretofore dominant party that on account of their persistence in maintaining the principles and sustaining the proceedings against which we have herein entered our solemn protest, we must and do hold them in disfellowship as a Church of Christ, and maintain that we only, and all who coincide with us, are entitled to the name "The First Baptist Church at Dallas, Texas," making our appeal to the world and brethren at large.

And now, dear brethren and sisters, we do kindly and affectionately invite all who believe as we do to unite with us, and thus aid in maintaining the right, and may God help the right.

J.L. Downs, Senior Deacon,
58 others at the time; about 80 now, Feb.

NOTES

Preface Note

1. *A History of Texas Baptists* (Dallas: Baptist Standard Publishing Co., 1923), p. 516.

Notes to Chapter One

1. Walter N. Vernon, Robert W. Sledge, Robert C. Monk, and Norman W. Spellman, *The Methodist Excitement in Texas* (Dallas: The Texas United Methodist Church Historical Society, 1984), 202–9.

2. Walter N. Vernon, *Methodism Moves Across North Texas* (Dallas: North Texas Conference Historical Society, 1967), 144–46.

3. Vernon, Sledge, Monk, and Spellman, 202–309.

4. Walter Prescott Webb, ed. *The Handbook of Texas*, 2 Vols. (Austin: Texas State Historical Association, 1952), s. v. "Christian Church," by W. W. Freeman.

5. William S. Speer and John H. Brown, eds., *Encyclopedia of the New West* (Marshall, TX: United States Biographical Publishing, 1881; reprint, Easley, SC: Southern Historical Press, 1978) s. v. "Samuel Augustus Hayden." See also W. E. Paxton, *A History of the Baptists of Louisiana from Earliest to the Present* (St. Louis: C. R. Barnes, 1888), 520–21.

6. Arthur W. Berger, *Guide to Louisiana Confederate Military Units, 1861–65* (Baton Rouge: Louisiana State University Press, 1989), 112.

7. William L. Thompson, "Captain S. A. Hayden as a Spy," *Confederate Veteran 5* (1897): 559.

8. No author, "Dr. S. A. Hayden," *Confederate Veteran 26* (1918): 533.

9. Keith L. Cogburn, "Samuel Augustus Hayden," in *The New Handbook of Texas* (Austin: Texas State Historical Society Press, 1996), 515.

10. S. A. Hayden, *The Complete Conspiracy Trial Book: Being An Historical, Philosophical, Ethical and Judicial Analysis of Eleven Baptist Lawsuits in Texas* (Dallas: The Texas Baptist Publishing House, 1907), 12.

11. Leon McBeth, *The First Baptist Church of Dallas: A Centennial History (1868–1968)* (Grand Rapids: Zondervan Publishing House, 1968), 79.

12. Hayden, *Complete Conspiracy,* 12.

13. *Church Minutes,* First Baptist Church of Dallas, 5 June, 1878. These minutes may be found in the serials department of the A. Webb Roberts Library at Southwestern Baptist Theological Seminary.

14. McBeth, *Dallas,* 74.

15. Karen Bullock, "The Life and Contributions of Robert Cooke Buckner: Progenitor of Organized Social Christianity Among Texas Baptists, 1860-1919" (Ph. D. diss.: Southwestern Baptist Theological Seminary, 1991), 60–61.

16. *Proceedings,* Baptist General Association of Texas, 1879, 27–31.

17. James Bodkin Link, *Historical and Biographical Magazine,* 2 vols. (Austin: n. p., 1892); reprint 4 vols. (Paris, AR: Baptist Standard Bearer, 1999), Vol. 4, 751.

18. B. F. Riley, *History of the Baptists of Texas: A Concise Narrative of the Baptist Denomination in Texas, from the Earliest Occupation of the Territory to the Close of the Year 1906* (Dallas: By the Author, 1907), 209.

19. Carl M. Suter, Jr., *O Zion Haste: The Story of the Dallas Baptist Association* (Dallas: Dallas Baptist Association, 1978), 51.

20. W. N. Griffeth, *Dallas Church Vindicated: Official Statement of Facts* (Dallas: Herald and Commercial Steam Printing House, 1880), 2-9.

21. Clerks Book, First Baptist Church of Dallas, 23.

22. Hayden, *Complete Conspiracy,* 13.

23. Griffeth, 3.

24. Bullock, 46–69; 77–82; 98. Buckner's lack of Landmark characteristics was also verified with Bullock via phone interview on July 12, 2004.

25. Oscar Davis, Mildred Ellis, and Louis W. Shepherd, *A History of First Baptist Church of Somerset, Kentucky, 1799–1974: One Hundred Seventy-Fifth Anniversary Edition* (Wolfe City, TX: Southern Baptist Press, 1974), 10.

26. James Robinson Graves, *Both Sides: A Full Investigation of the Charges Preferred Against Elder J. R. Graves* (Nashville: Spring Street Baptist Church, 1859), 234.

27. William Williams Keen, ed., *The Bicentennial Celebration of the Founding of the First Baptist Church of Philadelphia, 1698–1898* (Philadelphia: American Baptist Publishing Society, 1899), 66–68.

28. James Milton Carroll, *A History of Texas Baptists: Comprising a Detailed Account of Their Activities, Their Progress and Their Achievements* (Dallas: Baptist Standard Publishing Company, 1923), 282.

29. McBeth, *Dallas,* 77.

30. Joseph Martin Dawson, *A Century With Texas Baptists* (Nashville: Broadman Press, 1947), 30.

31. J. M. Carroll, *Texas Baptist Statistics, 1895* (Houston: J. J. Pastoriza Printing and Litho. Co., 1896; reprint, Dallas: Baptist General Convention of Texas Press, 1985), 8.

32. *Proceedings,* Baptist General Association of Texas, 1873, 15.

33. Riley, 221.

34. Leslie Robinson Elliott, *Centennial Story of Texas Baptists* (Dallas: Baptist General Convention of Texas, 1936), 45.

35. Dawson, 26.

36. D. R. Peveto, *The Union Baptist Association: Centennial History, 1840–1940* (n. c., n. p. 1940), 36–37.

37. L. L. Foster, *Forgotten Texas Census: First Annual Report of the Agricultural Bureau of the Department of Agriculture, Insurance, Statistics and History, 1887–88* (Austin: Texas State Historical Association, 2001), 229.

38. Suter, 312.

39. Foster, 153.

40. J. L. Walker and C. P. Lumpkin, *History of the Waco Baptist Association of Texas* (Waco: Byrne-Hill Printing House, 1897), 102–8.

41. Foster, 316.

42. Elliott, 45.

43. Carroll, *History,* 524–25.

44. Dawson, 27.

45. Leon McBeth, *Texas Baptists: A Sesquicentennial History* (Dallas: Baptistway Press, 1998), 84.

46. Carroll, *History,* 388, 525.

47. Link, Vol. 2, 244.

48. Carroll, *History,* 546.

49. Link, Vol. 2, 244.

50. Dawson, 29.

51. *Minutes of the Called Session—24 February 1880,* Baptist General Association of Texas, 1.

52. *Texas Baptist Herald,* 4 March 1880, 2.

53. J. B. Cranfill and J. L. Walker, *R. C. Buckner: Life of Faith and Works* (Dallas: Buckner Home Press, 1914), 111.

54. *Texas Baptist Herald,* 4 March 1880, 2.

55. Link, Vol. 4, 692.

56. B. H. Carroll, "Distinctive Baptist Principles: A Sermon Before the Pastor's Conference at Dallas, 4 November 1903," 9–14.

57. B. H. Carroll, *Christ and His Church,* eds. J. W. Crowder and J. B. Cranfill (Dallas: Helms Printing, Co., 1940), 83.

58. *Texas Baptist Herald,* 4 March 1880, 2.

59. McBeth, *Dallas,* 74.

60. Link, Vol. 1, 756.

61. *Minutes,* Elm Fork Baptist Association, May 1881.

62. Hayden, *Complete Conspiracy,* 12, 13.

63. McBeth, *Dallas,* 76–79.

64. Griffeth, 12.

65. *Minutes,* First Baptist Church of Dallas, 30 March 1883.

66. Cranfill and Walker, 111.

67. McBeth, *Dallas,* 80.

68. Robert Taylor Hanks, *Mrs. Mattie Bernard Hanks: The Preacher's Wife* (El Paso: n.p., n.d.), 16.

Notes to Chapter Two

1. Edward L. Ayers, Lewis L. Gould, David M. Oshinsky, and Jean R. Soderlund, *American Passages: A History of the United States* (New York: Harcourt College Publishers, 2000), 549–50.

2. Dawson, 28.

3. Carroll, *History*, 424–25.

4. Riley, 206.

5. Link, Vol. 4, 699.

6. Dawson, 36.

7. *Proceedings*, Baptist General Association of Texas, 1883, 26–28.

8. Robert A. Baker, *The Blossoming Desert: A Concise History* (Waco: Word Book Publishers, 1970), 146.

9. Carroll, *History*, 641.

10. *Proceedings*, Baptist General Association of Texas, 1885, 27–28.

11. Elliott, 52.

12. Carroll, *History*, 525.

13. Link, Vol. 4, 755. See also Dawson, 37.

14. Carroll, *History*, 580.

15. McBeth, *Texas*, 88.

16. *Minutes*, Baptist State Convention of Texas, 1885.

17. Riley, 296.

18. Carroll, *History*, 648.

19. *Proceedings*, Temple Meeting, 1885.

20. Ibid.

21. Ibid.

22. McBeth, *Texas*, 88.

23. Z. N. Morrell, *Flowers and Fruits in the Wilderness*, 4th ed. (Boston: Gould and Lincoln, 1886; reprint, Waco: Markham Press Fund of Baylor University Press, 1976), 428.

24. Link, Vol. 4, 469.

25. Carroll, *History*, 658.

26. *Proceedings*, Baptist General Convention of Texas, 1886, 23.

27. McBeth, *Texas*, 86.

28. Hayden, *Complete Conspiracy*, 18.

29. Glenn Jonas, "The Political Side of B. H. Carroll," in *Baptist History and Heritage* 33 (Autumn 1998): 49–55.

30. Robert A. Baker, *Tell The Generations Following: A History of Southwestern Baptist Theological Seminary, 1908–1983* (Nashville: Broadman Press, 1983), 121.

31. Ibid., 121–52.

32. Carroll, *History*, 660 n1.

33. *Texas Baptist and Herald*, 8 July 1886, 4.

34. McBeth, *Texas*, 181–82.

35. Carroll, *History*, 661.

Notes to Chapter Three

1. Rupert N. Richardson, Adrien Anderson, Cary D. Wintz, and Ernest Wallace, *Texas: The Lone Star State* (Upper Saddle River, NJ: Prentice Hall, 2001), 275.

2. Roy R. Barkley and Mark F. Odintz, eds., *The Portable Handbook of Texas* (Austin: The Texas State Historical Association, 2000): "Dallas" by Jackie McElhaney and Michael V. Hazel, 261–65.

3. Ibid., "Waco" by Roger N. Conger, 940.

4. Carroll, *History*, 661.

5. Suter, 61.

6. Hayden, *Complete Conspiracy*, 19, 351.

7. Elliott, 56.

8. James Britton Cranfill, *Dr. J. B. Cranfill's Chronicle, A Story of Life in Texas* (New York: Fleming H. Revell Co., 1916), 402.

9. Link, Vol 4, 469.

10. McBeth, *Texas*, 119.

11. Dawson, 54.

12. Carroll, *History*, 909.

13. Riley, 312–13; Dawson, 30; McBeth, *Texas*, 119; R. T. Hanks to J. M. Carroll, 29 January 1922, J. M. Carroll Collection, file 776, Archives, Southwestern Baptist Theological Seminary.

14. Link, Vol 4, 757–78.

15. Hayden, *Complete Conspiracy*, 313.

16. Reverend J. R. Clark, Statement, cited in Hayden, *Complete Conspiracy*, 313.

17. Dr. William Howard, Personal Statement, cited in Hayden, *Complete Conspiracy*, 313.

18. Elliott, 109.

19. McBeth, *Dallas*, 89.

20. Hanks, 16.

21. *Minutes*, First Baptist Church of Dallas, 17 April 1889.

22. Ibid.

23. Hayden, *Complete Conspiracy*, 312–13.

24. A. J. Holt and S. A. Hayden to B. H Carroll, 29 May 1889, file 251, B. H. Carroll Collection, Archives, Southwestern Baptist Theological Seminary; A. J. Holt and S. A. Hayden to B. H. Carroll, 3 June 1889, file 251, archives, Southwestern Baptist Theological Seminary.

25. McBeth, *Dallas*, 89.

26. Link, Vol. 4, 759.

27. Examples may be found in *Texas Baptist and Herald*, 5 June 1889, 8 (x); *Texas Baptist and Herald*, 12 June 1889, 5.

28. A. J. Holt, Letter, 13 August 1890. Cited in Hayden, *Complete Conspiracy*, 316–17.

29. E. E. Gibson, Herbert Morris, and Chas. I. Evans Sr. *The Hayden-Cranfill Conspiracy Trial: Stenographically Reported* (Dallas: Texas Baptist Publishing House, 1899), 40.

30. Statement of Twenty Baptist Ministers, 9 September 1890. Cited in Hayden, *Complete Conspiracy*, 317–18. See also *Texas Baptist and Herald*, 12 June 1889, 4 (x).

31. Hanks, 17.

32. Cranfill, *Dr. J. B. Cranfill's Chronicle*, 435.

Notes to Chapter Four

1. Barkley and Odintz, "Dallas."

2. Riley, 313.

3. Cranfill, 402.

4. Riley, 312–13.

5. E. C. Routh, *The Life Story of Dr. J. B. Gambrell* (Oklahoma City: Published by the Author, 1929), 62.

6. Link, Vol 4, 471.

7. Tom Berger, *Baptist Journalism in Nineteenth-Century Texas* (Austin: Texas Journalism Press, 1970), 59.

8. Elliot, 56.

9. *Texas Baptist Herald*, 29 January 1890, 10.

10. Link, Vol. 4, 472. Especially those Baptists in Dallas.

11. McBeth, *Texas*, 113.

12. Carroll, *Texas*, 722–24.

13. McBeth, *Texas*, 114–15.

14. B. F. Fuller, *A History of Texas Baptists* (Louisville: Baptist Book Concern, 1900), 398.

15. *Minutes* of Ex Parte Council Held at the Call of the Minority of the First Baptist Church, Paris, Texas, February 11 & 12, 1896 (Paris: P. H. Bennett, Printer, 1896), 12.

16. Carroll, *Texas*, 724.

17. McBeth, *Texas*, 118.

18. *Baptist Standard*, 20 May 1897, 12.

19. *Proceedings*, BGCT, 1897, 91.

20. Elliott, 118.

21. Link, Vol. 4, 472.

22. Hayden, *Complete Conspiracy*, 19.

23. Cited in Berger, 57.

24. Gambrell, *Evolution of the Texas Situation*. Cited in Riley, 347.

25. Dawson, 55.

26. Hayden, *Complete Conspiracy*, 20–21.

27. B. H. Carroll, Waco, to S. A. Hayden, Dallas, ALS, 5 December 1893, File 252 B. H. Carroll Collection.

28. Hayden, *Complete Conspiracy*, 21.

29. *Texas Baptist and Herald*, 18 January 1894, 4-5. (x)

30. Alan J. Lefever, *Fighting the Good Fight: The Life and Work of Benajah Harvey Carroll* (Austin: Eakin Press, 1994), 69.

31. Cranfill, *Chronicle*, 440.

32. Hayden, *Complete Conspiracy*, 20–23.

33. Cranfill, *Chronicle*, 425.

34. Riley, 364.

35. Cranfill, *From Memory*, 81–82.

36. Carroll, *History*, 708 n 2.

37. S. A. Hayden to J. M. Carroll, 26 May 1894, J. M. Carroll Collection, file 677, Archives, Southwestern Baptist Theological Seminary.

38. J. M. Carroll to S. A. Hayden, May 1894, J. M. Carroll Collection, file 671, Archives, Southwestern Baptist Theological Seminary.

39. Carroll, *History*, 692.

40. Dawson, 55.

41. *Proceedings*, Called Session of the Executive Board of the Baptist General Convention of Texas, 1894. Cited in Carroll, *History*, 688–92.

42. *Texas Baptist and Herald*, 13 October 1892, 1.

43. Frank E. Burkhalter, *A World-Visioned Church: Story of the First Baptist Church Waco, Texas* (Nashville: Broadman Press, 1946), 135.

44. Cranfill, *Chronicle*, 444–5.

45. Hayden, *Complete Conspiracy*, 307–9.

46. J. M. Carroll to J. B. Cranfill, 12 February 1896, file 755, J. M. Carroll Collection, Archives, Southwestern Baptist Theological Seminary.

47. Hayden, *Complete Conspiracy*, 60–75.

48. Riley, 364.

49. Cranfill, *Chronicle*, 434.

50. Riley, 365.

51. Hayden, *Complete Conspiracy*, 251.

Notes to Chapter Five

1. Carroll, *History*, 704.

2. *Proceedings*, Baptist General Convention of Texas, 1893. This quote is not recorded in the actual Proceedings. However, it is cited in Carroll's *History*, 707.

3. S. A. Hayden, *Letter to the Board Members of the BGCT*, 2 April 1894.

4. Hayden, *Complete Conspiracy*, 22.

5. *Minutes*, Called Session of the Board of the BGCT, 9 April 1894. Cited in Carroll, *History*, 710.

6. Hayden, *Complete Conspiracy*, 23.

7. The entire article is reprinted in *The Texas Baptist and Herald*, 19 April 1894; Hayden, *Complete Conspiracy*, 23–24.

8. Hayden, *Complete Conspiracy*, 23.

9. Carroll, *History*, 712.

10. Baker, *The Blossoming Desert*, 158.

11. *Minutes*, Called Session of the BGCT, 26–27 June 1894. Cited in Carroll, *History*, 714.

12. For example see, *Texas Baptist and Herald*, 4 October 1894, 1 (x). See also, John Heuthank to B. H Carroll, 14 September 1894, B. H. Carroll Collection, reel 4, serials, Southwestern Baptist Theological Seminary. Hayden was especially prone to resurrect this episode as it appeared in his *Complete Conspiracy Trial Book* as late as 1907. See page 259.

13. Baker, *The Blossoming Desert*, 158.

14. Cranfill and Walker, 160–61.

15. Riley, 365.

16. Cranfill, *Chronicle*, 441.

17. Baker, *The Blossoming Desert*, 158–59.

Notes to Chapter Six

1. Hayden, *Complete Conspiracy*, 128.

2. Cranfill to Burleson, 25 January 1895, B. H. Carroll Collection, file 228, Archives, Southwestern Baptist Theological Seminary.

3. Riley, 365.

4. Cranfill, *Chronicle*, 442.

5. *Proceedings*, Baptist General Convention of Texas, 1895, 7.

6. Ibid., 8.

7. Ibid., 7, 8.

8. J. M. Pendleton, *Church Manual: Designed for the Use of Baptist Churches* (Philadelphia: American Baptist Publication Society, 1867), 102.

9. Edward T. Hiscox, *The Baptist Church Directory: A Guide to the Doctrines and Discipline, Officers and Ordinances, Principles and Practices, of Baptist Churches. Embracing a Concise View of the Questions of Baptism and Communion* (New York: Sheldon and Company, 1860), 57.

10. *Proceedings*, Baptist General Convention of Texas, 1895, 36.

11. *Constitution*, Baptist General Convention of Texas.

12. Pendleton, *Church Manual*, 102.

13. Hiscox, *Church Directory*, 57.

14. Jesse C. Fletcher, *The Southern Baptist Convention: A Sesquicentennial History* (Nashville: Broadman and Holman Publishers, 1994), 83; James E. Tull, *A Study of Southern Baptist Landmarkism in the Light of Historical Ecclesiology*, Vol. 2 (New York: Columbia University Press, 1960), 638.

15. For an excellent overview of B. H. Carroll's ecclesiology see, James Spivey, "Benajah Harvey Carroll," in *Baptist Theologians*, eds., Timothy George and David Dockery (Nashville: Broadman and Holman Publishers, 1990), 318–19. B. H. Carroll maintained the Landmarkist tenets of: A visible Baptist, and not universal church; the sovereignty of the local church, no alien baptism, successionism, and no pulpit affiliations with non-Baptists.

16. J. M. Carroll, *The Trail of Blood* (Lexington, KY: Ashland Avenue Baptist Church, 1931).

17. J. B. Gambrell, *Ecclesiological Lectures* (Fort Worth: Southwestern Baptist Theological Seminary Archives, 1918–19); *Baptist Standard*, 3 December 1896, 1; *Baptist Standard*, 11 November 1897, 13; J. B. Gambrell, *Baptists and Their Business* (Nashville: Sunday School Board, 1919), 72–74. These works clearly demonstrate that Gambrell held to: a visible baptism, and not a universal church; the sovereignty of the local church, no alien baptism, successionism, and no pulpit affiliations with non-Baptists.

18. B. H. Carroll, *Baptists and Their Doctrines: Sermons on Distinctive Baptist Principles*, ed. J. B. Cranfill (Nashville: Broadman Press, 1913), 31.

19. Riley, 378.

20. Carroll, *History*, 732.

21. *Proceedings*, Baptist General Convention of Texas, 1896, 22–23.

22. Ibid.

23. Ibid., 22–36.

24. Riley, 382.

25. Carroll, *History*, 746.

26. Cranfill, *Chronicle*, 445.

27. *Proceedings*, Baptist General Convention of Texas, 1896, 24.

28. Carroll, *History*, 748.

29. Riley, 378.

30. R. C. Buckner to B. H. Carroll, 22 March 1897, file 173, B. H. Carroll Collection, Archives, Southwestern Baptist Theological Seminary.

31. Dawson, 60; Carroll, *History*, 749.

32. Dawson, 60–61.

33. McBeth, *Baptist Heritage*, 348.

34. Ibid., 416.

35. T. P. Crawford, *Churches to the Front*! (China: n. p., 1892).

36. Daniel Parker, *A Public Address to the Baptist Society, and Friends of Religion in General, on the Principle and Practice of the Baptist Board of Foreign Missions for the United States of America* (Vincennes, IN: Stout & Osborne, 1820), 46–47.

37. McBeth, *Texas*, 70.

38. *Texas Baptist Herald*, 2 September 1897, 1.

39. McBeth, *Texas*, 119; Baker, *The Blossoming Desert*, 157.

40. Hayden, *Complete Conspiracy*, 253. By "adequate cause," Hayden probably meant heresy.

41. Carroll, *History*, 596.

42. Baylor University, "Minutes of the Board of Trustees," 19 July 1897.

43. Carroll, *History*, 751.

44. William Cowper Brann, *The Complete Works of Brann the Iconoclast* (New York: The Brann Publishers, 1898), V. 1 (Feb., 1895); V. 2, (Mar., 1895); V. 4 (May, 1895).

45. *Waco Morning News*, 16 June, 1895, 5.

46. Ibid.

47. Brann, *The Iconoclast*, V. 6 (July, 1895).

48. Ibid, VII, 9 (Oct., 1897).

49. George W. Baines to B. H. Carroll, 19 July 1897, file 174, B. H. Carroll Collection, reel 4, Archives, Southwestern Baptist Theological Seminary.

50. A. S. Bunting to B. H. Carroll, 7 September 1897, file 217, B. H. Carroll Collection, Archives, Southwestern Baptist Theological Seminary.

51. Carroll, *History*, 751–52; *Baptist Standard*, 21 October 1897, 4–5.

52. Riley, 389–90.

53. Ibid., 392.

54. Carroll, *History*, 752.

55. *Proceedings*, Baptist General Convention of Texas, 1897, 99–101.

56. Ibid., 99–101.

57. Hayden, *Complete Conspiracy*, 146–48.

58. Cranfill, *Chronicle*, 454–56.

Notes to Chapter Seven

1. Carroll, *History*, 773.

2. Cranfill and Walker, 166.

3. *Proceedings*, Baptist General Convention of Texas, 1898, 11–24.

4. *Baptist Standard*, 13 October 1898, 1.

5. *Texas Baptist and Herald*, 12 October 1899, 1.

6. Constitution of the Baptist General Convention of Texas, cited in Fuller, 307.

7. Private Letter, E. B. Hardie to R. C. Buckner, 11 November 1899, Archives, Buckner Baptist Benevolences, Inc; Dallas, Texas. There is no evidence that indicates that Buckner held to Hayden's theories.

8. J. B. Gambrell to B. H. Carroll, 3 October 1899, file 443, B. H. Carroll Collection, Archives, Southwestern Baptist Theological Seminary.

9. Riley, 413.

10. Cranfill and Walker, 168.

11. *Proceedings*, Baptist General Convention of Texas, 1899, 12–14.

12. Cranfill and Walker, 168.

13. *Proceedings*, Baptist General Convention of Texas, 1899, 12.

14. Ibid., 12–17.

15. Carroll, *History*, 785.

16. *Proceedings*, Baptist General Convention of Texas, 1899, 17.

17. R. C. Vance, *A History of the B.M.A. of Texas From 1900 to 1953* (n.c., n.p., 1953), 11.

18. McBeth, *Dallas*, 134.

19. Carroll, *History*, 792 n 1.

20. W. H. Parks, *A History of the Baptist Missionary Association of Texas* (Cleburne, TX: Review, n.d.), 34. See also *Texas Baptist and Herald*, 30 November 1899, 1. In addition, Hayden again denies that he is a "Gospel Missions man."

21. *Proceedings*, Baptist General Convention of Texas, 1900, 13.

22. Riley, 422.

23. Carroll, *History*, 792; Vance, 15.

24. C. E. Colton, "Baptist Missionary Association," *Encyclopedia of the Southern Baptists*, Vol. 1 (Nashville: Broadman Press, 1958), 118–19.

25. Vance, 11.

26. Parks, 33.

27. Vance, 13.

28. Ibid., 19–20.

29. Ibid., 27.

30. McBeth, *Heritage*, 751–53.

31. W. W. Barnes, *The Southern Baptist Convention: 1845–1953* (Nashville: Broadman Press, 1954), 114–15.

32. Riley, 426.

33. Letter, From J. B. Cranfill to the First Baptist Church of Dallas, contained in the *Minutes* of the First Baptist Church of Dallas, 27 May 1904.

34. Hayden, *Complete Conspiracy*, 211–18.

35. Ibid. 146.

36. Routh, 69.

37. Cranfill, *Chronicle*, 456.

38. Dawson, 62.

39. Riley, 405.

Notes to Chapter Eight

1. McBeth, *Sourcebook*, 327.

2. Tull, Vol. 2, 638.

3. McBeth, *Texas*, 456.

4. Ibid.

5. *Plumbline*, December 1997, 8.

6. Ibid.

BIBLIOGRAPHY

Primary Sources

Buckner, Robert Cooke. "A Memorial." Presented to the First Baptist Church, Dallas, 24 December 1879. Original housed in Archives, A. Webb Roberts Library, Southwestern Baptist Theological Seminary.

Carroll, Benajah Harvey. *Christ and His Church.* Edited by J. W. Crowder and J. B. Cranfill. Dallas: Helms Printing, Co., 1940.

_________. "Distinctive Baptist Principles: A Sermon Before the Pastor's Conference at Dallas." 4 November 1903.

Carroll, James Milton. *A History of Texas Baptists: Comprising a Detailed Account of Their Activities, Their Progress and Their Achievements.* Dallas: Baptist Standard Publishing, 1923.

_________. *Texas Baptist Statistics, 1895.* Houston: J. J. Pastoriza Printing and Litho. Co., 1896; reprint, Dallas: Baptist General Convention of Texas Press, 1985.

_________. *The Trail of Blood.* Lexington, KY: Ashland Avenue Baptist Church, 1931.

Cranfill, James Britton. *From Memory: Reminiscences, Recitals, and Gleanings from a Bustling and Busy Life.* Nashville: Broadman Press, 1937.

_________. *Dr. J. B. Cranfill's Chronicle: A Story of Life in Texas.* New York: Fleming H. Revell Company, 1916.

Cranfill, J. B., and J. L. Walker. *R. C. Buckner: Life of Faith and Works.* Dallas: Buckner Home Press, 1914.

Crawford, T. P. *Churches to the Front!* China: n.p., 1892.

First Baptist Church, Dallas. *Dallas Church Defended.* Dallas: First Baptist Church, 1880.

———. Clerks Book.

Fuller, B. F. *History of Texas Baptists.* Louisville: Baptist Book Concern, 1900.

Gambrell, J. B. *Baptists and Their Business.* Nashville: Sunday School Board, 1919.

_________. *The Baptist General Convention of Texas and Its Work.* Dallas: Executive Board, Baptist General Convention of Texas, 1918.

_________. *Ecclesiological Lectures.* Fort Worth: Southwestern Baptist Theological Seminary Archives, 1918–19.

_________. *Ten Years in Texas.* Dallas: The Baptist Standard, 1910.

Gibson, E. E., Herbert Morris, and Chas. I. Evans Sr. *The Hayden-Cranfill Conspiracy Trial: Stenographically Reported.* Dallas: Texas Baptist Publishing House, 1899.

Griffeth, W. N. *Dallas Church Vindicated: Official Statement of Facts.* Dallas: Herald and Commercial Steam Printing House, 1880.

Hanks, R. T. *Mrs. Mattie Bernard Hanks: The Preacher's Wife.* El Paso: n. p., n. d.

Hayden, S. A. *The Complete Conspiracy Trial Book.* Dallas: The Texas Baptist Publishing House, 1907.

Link, John Bodkin. *Texas Historical and Biographical Magazine.* 4 Vols. Austin: n.p., 1892. Reprint, Paris, AR.: The Baptist Standard Bearer, 1999.

Morrell, Z. N. *Flowers and Fruits in the Wilderness*, 4th ed. Boston: Gould and Lincoln, 1886.

Parker, Daniel. *A Public Address to the Baptist Society, and Friends of Religion in General, on the Principle and Practice of the Baptist Board of Foreign Missions for the United States of America.* Vincennes, IN: Stout & Osborne, 1820.

Riley, B. F. *History of the Baptists of Texas: A Concise Narrative of the Baptist Denomination in Texas, From the Earliest Occupation of the Territory to the Close of the Year 1906.* Dallas: by the author, 1907.

Walker, J. L. and C. P. Lumpkin. *History of the Waco Baptist Association of Texas.* Waco: Byrne-Hill Printing House, 1897.

Secondary Works

Alan, Clifton, ed. *Encyclopedia of Southern Baptists.* 4 Vols. Nashville: Broadman Press, 1958.

Ayers, Edward L., Lewis L. Gould, David M. Oshinsky, and Jean R. Soderlund. *American Passages: A History of the United States.* New York: Harcourt College Publishers, 2000.

Baker, Robert A. *A Summary of Christian History.* Nashville: Broadman Press, 1959.

_________. *The Blossoming Desert: A Concise History of Texas Baptists.* Waco: Word Books Publisher, 1970.

_________. *The Southern Baptist Convention and Its People, 1607–1972.* Nashville: Broadman Press, 1974.

_________. *Tell the Generations Following: A History of Southwestern Baptist Theological Seminary, 1908–1983.* Nashville: Broadman Press, 1983.

Baptist General Convention of Texas, Centennial Committee. *Texas Baptist Family Album 1885-1918.* Dallas: Baptist General Convention of Texas, 1985.

Barnes, William Wright. *The Southern Baptist Convention, 1845-1953.* Nashville: Broadman Press, 1954.

Beck, Rosalie. "The Whitsitt Controversy: A Denomination in Crisis." Ph.D. diss., Baylor University, 1985.

Berger, Tom. *Baptist Journalism in Nineteenth-Century Texas.* Austin: Texas Journalism Press, 1970.

Burkhalter, Frank. *A World-Visioned Church: Story of the First Baptist Church Waco, Texas.* Nashville: Broadman Press, 1946.

Burleson, Georgia J. *The Life and Writings of Rufus C. Burleson.* np: by the author, 1901.

Bullock, Karen O'Dell. "The Life and Contributions of Robert Cooke Buckner; Progenitor of Organized Social Christianity Among Texas Baptists, 1860–1919." Ph.D. diss., Southwestern Baptist Theological Seminary, 1991.

Carroll, J. M. "The Story of My Life, Chapters One Through Sixteen." *Journal of Texas Baptist History* 6 (1986).

Cogburn, Keith Lynn. "B. H. Carroll and Controversy: A Study of Leadership Among Texas Baptists, 1871–1899." M.A. thesis, Baylor University, 1983.

_________. "Samuel Augustus Hayden," *The New Handbook of Texas,* Vol 3. Austin: State Historical Society Press, 1996.

Colton, C. E. "Baptist Missionary Association." *Encyclopedia of Southern Baptists*, Vol. 2. Nashville: Broadman Press, 1958.

Davis, Oscar, Mildred Ellis, and Louis W. Shepherd. *A History of First Baptist Church of Somerset, Kentucky, 1799-1974: One Hundred Seventy-Fifth Anniversary Edition.* Wolfe City, TX: Southern Baptist Press, 1974.

Dawson, Joseph Martin. *A Century With Texas Baptists.* Nashville: Broadman, 1947.

Detherage, May. *Highlights of History of First Baptist Church New Orleans: A Saga of Baptist Beginnings, Growth, and Labors For Christ in the Crescent City. The Story of a Church, Her Great Grandchildren, and Even Great Great Grandchildren.* N. p., 1968.

Driskill, Frank A. *Historic Churches of Texas: The Land and Its People.* Burnett, TX: Eakin Press, 1980.

Elliott, Leslie Robinson, ed. *Centennial Story of Texas Baptists.* Dallas: Baptist General Convention of Texas, 1936.

Ellison, Ronald C. *Texas and Baptist Sunday Schools, 1829–1996.* Austin: Eakin Press, 1997.

Fletcher, Jesse. *The Southern Baptist Convention: A Sesquicentennial History.* Nashville: Broadman and Holman Publishers, 1994.

Foster, L. L. *Forgotten Texas Census: First Annual Report of the Agricultural Bureau of the Department of Agriculture, Insurance, Statistics, and History, 1887-88.* Austin: Texas State Historical Association, 2001.

Graves, J. R. *Old Landmarkism: What is It?* Memphis, TN: Baptist Book House, Graves Mahaffy & Company, 1880.

__________. *Both Sides: A Full Investigation of the Charges Preferred Against Elder J. R. Graves.* Nashville: Spring Street Baptist Church, 1859.

Harris, Lawrence Holiday. *The Origins and Growth of Baptist Faith: Twenty Baptist Trailblazers in World History.* Spartanburg, SC: The Reprint Company Publishers, 2001.

Hiscox, Edward T. *The Baptist Church Directory: A Guide to the Doctrines and Discipline, Officers and Ordinances, Principles and Practices, of Baptist Churches. Embracing A Concise View of the*

Questions of Baptism and Communion. New York: Sheldon and Company, 1860.

Hudson, Winthrop S. ed. *Baptist Concepts of the Church.* Chicago: Judson Press, 1959.

Keen, William Williams, ed. *The Bicentennial Celebration of the Founding of the First Baptist Church of Philadelphia, 1698–1898.* Philadelphia: American Baptist Publishing Society, 1899.

Lefever, Alan J. *Fighting the Good Fight: The Life and Work of Benajah Harvey Carroll.* Austin: Eakin Press, 1994.

Mason, Zane Allen. *Frontiersman of the Faith: A History of Baptist Pioneer Work in Texas.* San Antonio: The Naylor Company, 1970.

McBeth, H. Leon. *The First Baptist Church of Dallas: A Centennial History.* Grand Rapids: Zondervan Publishing House, 1968.

_________. *The Baptist Heritage: Four Centuries of Baptist Witness.* Nashville: Broadman Press, 1987.

_________. *Texas Baptists: A Sesquicentennial History.* Dallas: Baptistway Press, 1998.

_________. *A Sourcebook For Baptist Heritage.* Nashville: Broadman Press, 1990.

McConnell, F. M. *The Agreement and Differences Between the Two Baptist General Bodies in Texas.* Dallas: Irwin, n.d.

Moser, M. L., and J. A. Scarboro. *The Bible, The Baptists and the Board System.* Little Rock, AR: The Challenge Press, 1975.

Murray, Lois Smith. *Baylor at Independence.* Waco: Baylor University Press, 1972.

Parks, W. H. *A History of the Baptist Missionary Association of Texas.* Cleburne, TX: Review, n.d.

Pendleton, J. M. *Church Manual: Designed for the Use of Baptist Churches.* Philadelphia: American Baptist Publication Society, 1867.

Peveto, D. R. *The Union Baptist Association: Centennial History, 1840–1940.* N. p., 1940.

Price, J. M. *Southwestern Men and Their Messages.* Kansas City: Central Seminary Press, 1948.

Ray, Jeff. *B. H. Carroll.* Nashville: The Sunday School Board of the Southern Baptist Convention, 1927.

Richardson, Rupert N., Adrien Anderson, Cary D. Wintz, and Ernest Wallace. *Texas: The Lone Star State.* Upper Saddle River, NJ: Prentice Hall, 2001.

Routh, E. C. *The Life Story of Dr. J. B. Gambrell.* Oklahoma City: By the author, 1929.

Speer, William S., and John H. Brown, eds. *Encyclopedia of the New West.* Marshall, TX: United States Biographical Publishing, 1881. Reprint, Easley, SC: Southern Historical Press, 1978. S.v." Samuel Augustus Hayden."

Spivey, James. "Benajah Harvey Carroll." In *Baptist Theologians.* Edited by Timothy George and David Dockery, 307–29. Nashville: Broadman and Holman Publishers, 1990.

Storrs, William G. "The Life and Work of J. M. Carroll." Ph.D. diss., Southwestern Baptist Theological Seminary, 1995.

Suter, Carl M. *O Zion Haste: The Story of the Dallas Baptist Association.* Dallas: Dallas Baptist Association, 1978.

Timmerman, N. D. "The Hayden-Cranfill Controversy." Th.D. thesis, Southwestern Baptist Theological Seminary, 1936.

Tull, James E. *A Study of Southern Baptist Landmarkism in the Light of Historical Ecclesiology.* 2 Vols. New York: Columbia University Press, 1960.

Tyler, Ron, Douglas Barnett, Roy Barkley, Penelope Anderson, and Mark Ordintz, eds. *The New Handbook of Texas.* 6 Vols. Austin: State Historical Society Press, 1996.

Vance, R. C. *A History of the BMA of Texas From 1900 to 1953.* Livingston, TX: Scott's Print Shop, n.d.

Vernon, Walter N., Robert W. Sledge, Robert C. Monk, and Norman W. Spellman, *The Methodist Excitement in Texas.* Dallas: The Texas United Methodist Church Historical Society, 1984.

Vernon, Walter N. *Methodism Moves Across North Texas.* Dallas: North Texas Conference Historical Society, 1967.

Webb, Walter Prescott, ed. *The Handbook of Texas.* 3 Vols. Austin: The Texas State Historical Association, 1952.

White, Michael A. *The History of Baylor University, 1845–1861.* Waco: Texian Press, 1968.

Wood, Presnall H., and Floyd W. Thatcher. *Prophets With Pens.* Dallas: Baptist Standard Publishing Company, 1969.

Periodicals

These periodicals may be found in the serials department of the A. Webb Roberts Library at Southwestern Baptist Theological Seminary.

Jonas, Glenn. "The Political Side of B. H. Carroll." *Baptist History and Heritage*, no. 3 (1998): 49–56.

The Missionary Worker. (Dallas, Texas). 1896–1999.

The Baptist Standard (Dallas, Texas). 1892–1899.

The Iconoclast (Waco, Texas). 1895–1898.

The Texas Baptist (Dallas, Texas). 1870–1886.

The Texas Baptist Herald (Houston and Dallas, Texas). 1865–1886.

The Texas Baptist and Herald (Dallas, Texas). 1886–1899.

The Waco Morning News (Waco, Texas). 1895.

This periodical may be found at the Fort Worth Public Library.

Confederate Veteran. (Wilmington, North Carolina). 1879, 1918.

Annuals, Minutes, and Proceedings Consulted

These works may be found in the serials department of the A. Webb Roberts Library at Southwestern Baptist Theological Seminary.

Baptist General Association. *Proceedings.* 1873–1885.

Baptist General Convention of Texas. *Book of Reports 1990.* Dallas: Baptist General Convention of Texas.

Baptist General Convention of Texas. *Proceedings.* 1886–1900.

Elm Fork Association. *Minutes.* 1877–1897.

First Baptist Church of Dallas. *Minutes.* 1878–1904.

Texas Baptist State Convention. *Minutes.* 1848–1885.

Collections Consulted

R. C. Buckner Collection. Archives, A. Webb Roberts Library, Southwestern Baptist Theological Seminary.

R. C. Buckner Collection. Archives, Buckner Baptist Benevolences, Dallas, Texas.

B. H. Carroll Collection. Archives, A. Webb Roberts Library, Southwestern Baptist Theological Seminary, Fort Worth, Texas.

J. M. Carroll Collection. Archives, A. Webb Roberts Library, Southwestern Baptist Theological Seminary, Fort Worth, Texas.

J. B. Gambrell Collection. Archives, A Webb Roberts Library, Southwestern Baptist Theological Seminary, Fort Worth, Texas.

INDEX